AN

EDUCATED

DECISION

ONE APPROACH TO THE VACCINATION
PROBLEM USING HOMOEOPATHY

by

Christina J Head, MCH, RS.Hom

D1421852

AN EDUCATED DECISION

One approach to the vaccination problem using Homoeopathy

I would like to stress that this is "one approach" to dealing with childhood immunisations. There are many ways of using homoeopathy and other homeopaths may have their own methods which are equally valid.

Christina Head and colleagues currently work at

The Lavender Hill Homoeopathic Centre, London SW11 1PJ

Christina J. Head MCH RsHom
PO Box 141
Reigate
Surrey RH2 9YT
Tel: 01737 762497

With grateful thanks to Chris Harris for patiently typing and re-typing this script, to Linda Allan for compiling the diagram of the immune system and to Kate Tilley for the wonderful front cover.

Published by the Lavender Hill Publishing Company
First edition 1995
Second edition 1999

AN EDUCATED DECISION
Vaccinations and Homoeopathy

CONTENTS

This book is dedicated to Maharaji
who continues to teach me to be humble:

"It's better to be humble.
To me humility is like that smoothness on an
aeroplane. You look at something really sleek.
It doesn't have those sharp corners and edges
and this and that. It's just sleek ~ that's like
humility ~ it allows no drag ~ it just lets it
happen."

Maharaji speaking to people in Miami,
Florida 1998.

www.maharaji.org

AN EDUCATED DECISION

INTRODUCTION

I have been working with children for 15 years and have treated all types of illnesses, physical and emotional. I have also treated many women during pregnancy and labour, with follow-up care of mother and baby. During this time, many parents came to me who have already investigated the current NHS vaccination programme in the UK and made a clear decision *not* to vaccinate their children. These parents came to me looking for an alternative way of dealing with their children's health and for support in their decision not to use the orthodox methods of disease prevention.

Parents have so many questions about this highly controversial subject, it requires more explanation than time in the consulting room allows, hence the birth of this book. It is written to answer your questions and provide you with the information you need to have a better understanding of homoeopathy and the importance of the immune system, and to show you that *you can* make educated decisions about vaccinations if you so wish.

Unvaccinated children cope with infection and disease in a very straightforward and simple manner. Generally they get less infections than vaccinated children, and respond more rapidly and successfully to medicines. Most unvaccinated children are *extremely* healthy and rarely become seriously ill, but given the myriad of individuals and individual circumstances, just being unvaccinated does not necessarily mean that a child will attain superhealth.

Homoeopathy is extremely effective in removing inherited diseases and bringing the whole person into balanced and positive health. In order to help you better understand it, below is a brief description of how homoeopathy was developed, how the remedies are made, and how this remarkable system of medicine works.

Like cures like

Homoeopathy was developed in the mid-1750s by a German doctor called Samuel Hahnemann, who was a well-respected physician with a busy and successful medical practice. However, after several years as a GP, he withdrew completely from medicine on the grounds that the practices of the time were killing more people than they cured! Instead, he made his living by translating documents and books (Hahnemann could read and write fluently in 12 languages!) During this time, he began to develop the system of medicine now known as homoeopathy.

By translating and studying old books, he became inspired to experiment with different ways of using medicines. He began by giving himself material[1] doses of Chinchona bark (commonly known as quinine), which is still used today as a medicine for malaria. However, he found taking material doses of substances can have severe, even life-threatening, side-effects, and when he took the Chinchona bark Hahnemann became quite ill with a typical malarial fever. This led him to the realisation that any substance given to a healthy person may, in a material dose, cause the disease that it can also treat when given in a Homoeopathic form, thus formulating the first rule of homoeopathy "like cures like". These dangerous side-effects are obviously not acceptable, so to make his medicines safe and gentle he invented the system of dilution and succussion.

Changing matter into energy
Dilution means adding water, or water and alcohol, to the original substance. Succussion is a process of shaking and banging the tube of liquid against the heel of the hand or a book: Hahnemann used a bible. Today most pharmacies use a machine, but the best remedies are still those made by hand.

To make the remedy, the Chinchona bark is first soaked and macerated in water and alcohol to preserve it and to allow its qualities to be absorbed into the mixture. Then one drop of this solution is added to ninety-nine drops of pure water and succussed one hundred times. One drop of this solution is then added to ninety-nine drops of pure water and again succussed one hundred times. This process is continued many many times until the required potency or strength is reached. It becomes so dilute that when tested in the laboratory, no trace of the original substance can be found.

What actually happens by using this method of dilution and succussion is that the original material is transformed from its material state into a fine energy pattern.

The remedies are then tested on healthy people by using a trial group, usually comprising one hundred people. Half of them are given a placebo and the

---

[1]The actual substance – not yet diluted or succussed.

other half the remedy, which is taken consistently over a period of time. During this trial period each person records the symptoms that he or she experiences on all levels: emotional, mental and physical. The symptoms that recur in the greatest number of people are recorded, and when this has been done many times an accurate picture evolves of what that medicine can do. What it can cause, it can also cure!

Doctors and scientists tend to view homoeopathy as "faith healing" or as having "a placebo effect". Basically, they are adopting the wrong approach. Certainly, if you try to examine a homoeopathic remedy under a microscope you will find nothing as the original substance has been enormously diluted. Some scientists have recently published a document relating to experiments done with different homoeopathic remedies in water. They found a definite energy pattern for each remedy. This has given homoeopathy at least some credibility within the scientific world, even though it has been tried and tested over and over and over for the last 250 years. Homoeopathy is the transfer of matter into energy, which is why it is so safe.

The germ has been blamed long enough
In the past, when most people lived in squalid and overcrowded conditions, when there were no sewers or drains, when the benefits of common hygiene were unknown of, and when wars and malnutrition were commonplace, it was not surprising that plagues and devastating infectious diseases wiped out thousands of people of all ages. This was the case in Europe at the turn of the 20th century, and in some countries still is today. The scientists of the time made a huge breakthrough in the discovery of germs and the subsequent education of people into the benefits of keeping clean.

However, the germ has been blamed long enough and it is time to move forward into the 21st century with a better understanding of the health and susceptibility of the individual as the underlying cause of disease rather than the germ. Hahnemann himself campaigned ceaselessly on matters of public health and hygiene, and was one of the first doctors to recognise the importance of cleanliness in relation to sound health.

In the more affluent nations of the world there are now good sewers and drainage, a relatively high standard of living for most of the population, much better nutrition, no wars, at least in western Europe for several decades, and good state education and medicine available to everyone. Why then, when you look around any school playground, do you see grey congested faces, children with permanent colds, coughs, tonsillitis, ear infections, and hyperactive or underactive energy?

What actually happens when a two-month-old baby is given several diseases and has to cope with them? Why are our children not in the peak of health and glowing with vitality and intelligence? Why do one in every three people die of cancer in our society? Why have ME, candidiasis and AIDS become so commonplace in the last forty years?

These are some of the many questions that people commonly ask and I hope that by the time you have finished reading this book you will have at least some of the answers – enough, I hope, to make your own "Educated Decision".

CHAPTER ONE

TO VACCINATE OR NOT?

The British government strongly advocates mass vaccination as the way to eliminate childhood diseases. This directive is forcefully presented to parents through their local clinics, GPs and health workers as the only way to ensure that their children remain healthy as they grow. It is one way of dealing with the problem, but not the only way.

Unfortunately, the medical establishment can be, and often is, very blinkered when it comes to new ideas. Parents who do not want to vaccinate their children are made to feel guilty, irresponsible and uncaring, and are often branded by their GPs as "difficult". They are told that if they do not vaccinate their children, they will be responsible for causing future epidemics which will affect the health of the children of all those "responsible" parents who did vaccinate. The government has even gone to the lengths of financially penalising GPs who do not get a certain percentage of vaccinations completed in their community. The pressure on parents to have these vaccinations done is enormous. The arguments put forward are frightening and damning at the same time, and it takes a strong person to say "no" to the orthodox methods.

Homoeopathy is not widely recognised as a complete system of medicine, and very few GPs have any knowledge or understanding of it. They consider that the decision not to vaccinate children is wrong and I certainly agree that to do nothing is asking for trouble. However, by using homoeopathy as an alternative, you are doing a lot *yourself* to care for your child.

Orthodox medicine is mass medicine. It is very effective, but it takes the responsibility away from the parents. Alternative medicine requires a lot of thought, understanding, and a high degree of responsibility on the part of the parents. It is a matter of choice which system you prefer to work with, though you can, of course, work with both.

However, in addition to all the stresses and strains of modern living, particularly if you have a large family, you may not wish to take on the added pressure of investigating and deciding whether or not to vaccinate your children. Also, homoeopathy is much more complicated to use than orthodox medicine, and much less widely available.

Side-effects of vaccination
It is rare that children die of the side-effects of vaccinations, but it does happen. The side-effects vary in severity according to the individual and the less dramatic effects mostly go unrecorded, or are put down to some other cause. Common minor side-effects include thrush, foot and mouth disease, repeated, painless ear infections, sleeplessness, aggressive behaviour, allergies, inability to concentrate and many more. These symptoms point to an underfunction or overfunction of the immune system, which is where the vaccinations do the most damage.

Chapters Three, Four and Five clearly set out the symptoms of all the childhood diseases which are presently vaccinated against plus some homoeopathic remedies that are useful during an infection. Every symptom of the disease itself can also be triggered by the vaccination, and this is where the dangers of mass immunisation, without regard to individual weakness, lie.

In the UK it is completely legal not to vaccinate, although most people do not realise this. In most countries of the world, children cannot attend school until they have had their quota of immunisations. It is heartening to know that the UK still leads the way in human rights, and that the individual can make a free choice.

In Germany also it is optional to vaccinate, although highly recommended by the medical profession, but the BCG is only done if the patient lives in a high-risk area. Recommended vaccination procedure is much the same as in the UK with the DPT, Polio and Hib being done after the age of 3 months.

In Switzerland (historically, the most health-conscious country in the world) only Polio is compulsory and children cannot attend school without it. All the others are optional and done at much the same ages as in the UK, except for Hib, which they do not use at all.

In New Zealand, the vaccination programme is also optional but strongly recommended. They have combined the DPT with Hib to make it into one shot, and also inoculate against hepatitis B at approximately 15 months. They aim to cover nine childhood diseases before the child is two years old.

In Australia, also, the vaccination programme is not compulsory but strongly recommended. The programme follows much the same pattern as in the UK, except that the DPT and Hib are done again at 18 months, and Aborigines and

Torres Strait Islanders are recommended to have Hepatitis B and the BCG at birth.

In Canada it is not compulsory but, again, highly recommended and the schedule is much the same as in the UK except that the DPT, Hib and Polio are all done again at 18 months.

In America and France, however, the vaccination programme is totally compulsory and children cannot attend school without proof of immunisation. In America the programme varies a little from state to state, and is done in a similar way to the UK. The American government has very recently introduced a compulsory vaccination against chicken pox and in some states also hepatitis B.

France recently stopped using the Hep B vaccine, having used it for 4 years, because of fears of neurological damage such as multiple sclerosis

What one is looking for from the consciousness of future generations is a respect for free choice, so, if you do choose to follow medical trends, that is your prerogative. Don't feel guilty either way!

What causes disease?
To help you understand the disease process, it is worth looking first at the fundamental differences of opinion regarding the actual cause of disease.

The commonly held belief in our society is that we are surrounded by antagonistic bacteria and viruses, whose sole purpose is to attack human beings and cause them untold misery and suffering. The orthodox approach is to remove these virulent organisms by counter-attack, i.e. using antibiotics, anti-inflammatory drugs, anti-protozoal drugs, anti-viral drugs and so on.

However, germs and viruses in themselves do not cause disease, but are a secondary reaction in an already weak system of the body. Certain germs and viruses are actually part of the healing process, as they initiate sanitation of the affected area. If removed, the original disease may become more chronic, or manifest as a more serious disease elsewhere in the body.

An example of how we confuse the cause of disease with the method of recovery can be seen by looking at the behaviour of some of the natural scavengers of our world. Rats and flies, for example, are branded as the carriers and causes of many terrible diseases. They are shunned, hated and feared, but if there were no rubbish, the rats and flies would not appear as there would be nothing for them to eat. Where there is rubbish, rats and flies initiate the process of decomposition that will eventually lead to a complete sanitation of the area. They are secondary to the initial problem, not the cause of it. To blame rats and flies for the existence of the rubbish would be illogical, to say the least, and to eliminate them simply leaves us with the original problems. Surely, it is far better either not to allow the rubbish to gather in the first place, or to remove the rubbish by sound and creative means.

We can see a parallel to this phenomenon in the human body. If it is looked after, cared for and loved, given nourishing food and kept clean, then the germs and viruses will not get a foothold. So, if germs and viruses do not, in fact, cause the disease, but are secondary to it, what actually does cause it?

Here, I should like to introduce the concept of *susceptibility*. *Susceptibility* of the individual, a weakness of any system of the body, whether inherited or acquired, and on any level: mental, emotional or physical.

Let us consider, for example, a baby born with a genetic weakness, such as an inherited allergy to cow's milk, which causes a tendency to produce catarrh. In addition to this, the child has a difficult birth, and its skull is compressed in the birth canal, or it has to be pulled out by forceps, thereby narrowing or changing the shape of the sinus passages (a very common scenario). The child will rapidly begin to produce repeated and painful infections in whatever area the catarrh collects: the middle ear, the nose, the sinus cavities, eustachian tubes, etc.

The orthodox treatment for this is antibiotics. These work quickly and effectively by removing the bacterial secondary infection, relieving the pain and appearing to cure the disease. However, all that has been done is to remove the secondary symptoms caused by the child's immune system trying to clear the infected catarrh. The inherited and/or acquired *susceptibility* is still there and is the true, underlying cause of the child's malaise.

If antibiotics are continued over several years (again, a common scenario), the catarrh continues to build up in, for example, the middle ear, with bacteria or viruses being attracted to the area in order to initiate the cleansing process and causing repeated infections. These repeated infections lead to a build-up of scar tissue on the tonsils, causing them to become permanently swollen. This in turn narrows the throat, and further complicates any ear problem by blocking the eustachian tubes, which run from the back of the mouth to the ear and are designed partly to drain catarrh away from the ears. If the underlying susceptibility is still not dealt with, the next step is an operation, either to remove the tonsils or adenoids, or both, or to have grommets (small, rubber rings) inserted into the ear drum in order to drain the ears of the catarrh. Wherever catarrh gathers, it will eventually attract bacteria or viruses in order to initiate the decomposition process.

As with the example of the rats and flies, the bacteria and viruses are attracted by their need for food. They are not the cause of the problems, but the process of decomposition and sanitation is very messy and can be damaging. The main problem with repeated infections that are left untreated or go on for too long, is that the inflammation spreads to eat away at the surrounding tissue or bone. In the case of repeated ear infections, for example, the inflammation may eat through the skull into the brain – a very nasty business indeed. This is where the skill of the doctor is paramount. A good doctor knows when to step in and clear the area with whatever means are to hand and remove the secondary infection if it is threatening to overtake the system. Antibiotics can perform a useful role in this way, but that is definitely not the end of the story.

Inherited and acquired susceptibility
The underlying *susceptibility* must also be dealt with, and here homoeopathy excels in creating good health by strengthening inherited or acquired weaknesses. I have had many children brought to me with exactly this problem. They have had repeated ear infections, repeated doses of antibiotics, but the problem is getting more and more serious because the focus is placed on the bacteria as the cause of the disease and the underlying *susceptibility* is completely ignored. This is so misleading that the child may end up having one or several operations, with general anaesthetic, and yet be left with a lifelong chronic sinus problem as the tendency to create catarrh is, still there. The underlying problem has never been addressed at all.

It is exactly the same with the infectious childhood diseases. It is very misleading to blame bacteria or viruses for causing these diseases. Where there is a *susceptibility*, bacteria or viruses are attracted by their need to live in favourable conditions and the immune system uses the secondary infection to initiate sanitation and to strengthen that particular weakness.

Once a disease has taken hold, it is the role of the doctor to decide whether or not the immune system is strong enough to deal with the disease or whether it needs help. However, with homoeopathy, the underlying *susceptibility* is looked at before the child becomes ill and, by using this *creative* medicine, such infections should never become serious.

Some of you may remember the flu holidays in the 1950s. People were offered a free week's holiday in the country in exchange for being "guinea pigs" in an experiment to find out why people caught the "common cold". They were exposed to all sorts of flu and cold viruses, but very few people actually developed a cold or flu! The scientists were disappointed and the experiment was abandoned.

Why did so few people become ill when they were heavily bombarded with germs and viruses? Probably because they were on holiday, they were relaxed and it was all a bit of fun. They were not *susceptible* at that point. Back in their normal environment, rushing to work in the cold and rain, and then going into a warm working environment with colleagues already infectious, they became *susceptible* and caught whatever germ or virus was going around. This is *susceptibility*.

Colds and flu are brought on by the results of overwork, stress, grief, exhaustion, etc. It is very often the end results of such stresses that suppress the immune system and make the person more *susceptible* to their environment.

This is really where the trouble lies. If a child is particularly *susceptible* to a certain disease, for example, whooping cough, he or she is automatically more *susceptible* to the side-effects of the whooping cough vaccination. This is why some children do not seem to react at all to the vaccinations, and some children react strongly, even fatally. In the next chapter, the effects of vaccination on the child's immune system is discussed more fully.

In 1808, Hahnemann treated and recorded in great detail a terrible epidemic of scarlet fever that was killing thousands of people at the time. He discovered that the deadly nightshade plant, otherwise known as *Belladonna*, made into a homoeopathic remedy, cured or lessened the strength of this terrible disease very effectively. He also experimented with this remedy by giving it to members of the family who had not yet contracted the disease. To his amazement this also worked, and not only did his system of medicine effectively cure the disease, but it also proved to act effectively as a prophylactic. This was the first true use of preventive medicine, well before Beauchamp and Pasteur developed the germ theory and vaccinations.

It is possible to use homoeopathy as a prophylaxis for any infectious disease. It can be recommended when travelling abroad, using the same principles as for the childhood diseases. However, that is another story.

If a child is brought to me by parents expressing a wish not to vaccinate in the orthodox way I look first at his or her health in as much detail as possible. Then carefully look at the family history as far as possible and deal with any symptoms that the child has at the time. When the child is well I give the parents a homoeopathic remedy made from each disease and ask them to administer one weekly to their child these remedies are called "Nosodes".

I have been using this method now with unvaccinated babies for the last eight years and so far the results have been extremely positive. It does mean, however, that the parents have to invest a lot of time and energy in learning about homoeopathy. They also have to deal with the ignorance of the medical profession and be prepared to take responsibility for their child's health. This has a minor effect of strengthening areas of the body that would be affected by that particular disease. However it is the careful use of constitutional, strenghtening treatment that will prevent the child from having serious side effects from a childhood disease. The use of Nosodes is an aid and is purely optional. More and more people are wanting to do this and, for those people, this system of preventive medicine is extremely beneficial.

Making choices
However, not everyone can be so purist in their approach and homoeopathy can be used in a "complementary" way to orthodox medicine. It is possible to give a homoeopathic remedy made from the actual vaccination itself before and after having the conventional inoculation. This helps to eliminate the side-effects, but does not seem as effective as not vaccinating at all. It is another approach, which combines both systems of medicine.

Whichever method you choose, it is your choice whether to go for the mass, uncomplicated vaccination programme with its possible risks, or to go for the homoeopathic approach by strengthening the individual.

I was prompted to consider the question of mass vaccination by the enormous number of children who came to me for treatment with vague symptoms and low-grade illnesses that would not respond to any type of medicine, including homoeopathy. These included persistent coughs and colds, dry coughs which resembled whooping cough but without any pathology, eczema and asthma that would not respond to well indicated remedies, and a host of other symptoms.

After careful thought, I concluded that the one thing all these children had in common was that they had all been vaccinated! Could this be the problem? In order to find out, I started experimenting by clearing the vaccinations first before giving any type of constitutional treatment and the results were astounding. So many children responded to this treatment that I had to conclude that the vaccinations were acting as a drug layer over the normal health of the individual and were somehow blocking the action of all types of medicine, as well as the normal functioning of the immune system.

Post-vaccination cleansing
In the last eight years I have also been following a procedure of routinely clearing out the side-effects of any vaccination a child may have had, before embarking upon constitutional homoeopathic treatment. So, when a child is brought to me for the first time, I initially go back through their vaccination history and undo any blocks that have occurred in the immune system through the vaccinations. For example, in the case of a two-year-old who has had MMR, DPT, Hib and Polio, I would give a dose of the MMR made into a homoeopathic remedy in the 200th strength, a week later a single dose of DPT 200; a week later a single dose of Polio 200, and a further week later a single dose of Hib 30. Any reactions are noted by the parent and in this way it can be clearly seen which vaccinations did the most damage. If a child is older then I do the same thing, but using stronger doses of the same remedies. Sometimes there is no particular reaction and sometimes the reaction is dramatic. In at least 30 per cent of all childhood cases this is enough to bring the child back to *perfect* health and they need no further treatment!

There is a tremendous value in doing this routine clearing in small children. I have noticed, since doing it, that my cure time has gone down from nine months to three months and it is much easier to see the child's true remedy after the immune system has been cleared. Children in our society are growing up with this "drug layer?", similar to someone using any drug (the pill, cortisones, etc.) and until this block is cleared it is often very difficult to see a true picture of the health of that individual.

In older children, I would go to very high doses of the homoeopathic equivalent of any vaccinations received in the past. Even with teenagers I notice that many of their problems start or are exacerbated by the BCG vaccination they have at thirteen or fourteen years. If you clear out the BCG very often their problems disappear, or the case becomes much clearer and easier to treat. This clearing is well worth doing, and my message to homoeopaths is to try it. You will see much more effective and quicker cures.

All the vaccinations also have the added complication of being laced with other substances designed to disinfect, enhance their action or help bind them together. The worst of these substances, in terms of toxicity, are thimerosal (derived from mercury), formaline (derived from formaldehyde), aluminium hydroxide, aluminium sulphate, aluminium phosphate, and calcium phosphate.

When looking at the side-effects of vaccination it is also worth keeping in mind the possible toxic effects of these substances. Sometimes after using the homoeopathic system of removing these side-effects, as described above, it may still be necessary to clear remaining problems with other appropriate homoeopathic remedies, such as Alumina or Mercury where symptoms suggest this is necessary.

Finally, I have to mention that these vaccinations are made from animal tissue, mainly from monkeys, rats, cattle, chickens and rabbits and then tested on them. Millions of animals are tortured and killed world-wide each year to provide us with this "protection". For more information on this read Jamie Murphy's book *What Every Parent Should Know About Childhood Vaccination,* listed at the back of this book.

How can any true healing come from the torture of innocent beings. How can medicine go forward into the 21st century with such blatant disregard for life itself?

THE IMMUNE SYSTEM

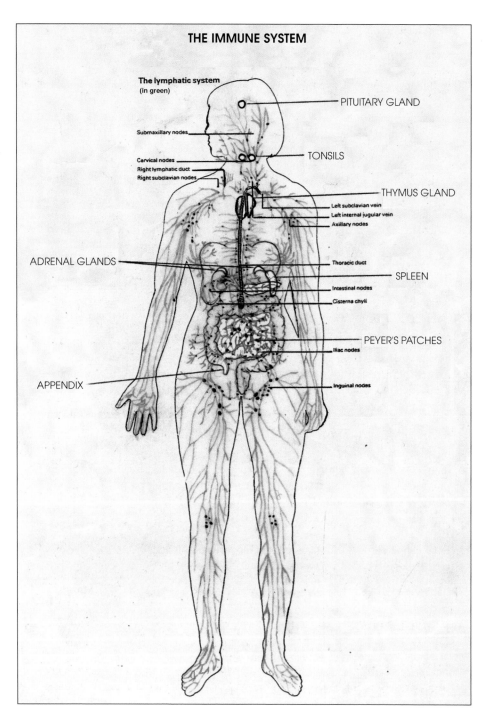

The lymphatic system
(in green)

PITUITARY GLAND

Submaxillary nodes

Cervical nodes
Right lymphatic duct
Right subclavian nodes

TONSILS

THYMUS GLAND

Left subclavian vein
Left internal jugular vein
Axillary nodes

ADRENAL GLANDS

Thoracic duct

SPLEEN

Intestinal nodes
Cisterna chyli

PEYER'S PATCHES

Iliac nodes

APPENDIX

Inguinal nodes

CHAPTER TWO

THE IMMUNE SYSTEM

The immune system is made up of complex, interactive cells working within a sophisticated network of vessels that cover the whole body. It is designed to keep the body clean and free of infection and disease. It is part of the miracle of life that, even in our most inspired moments, we do not fully comprehend. When the individual suffers illness or accident the huge resources of this system clean and repair in a pre-programmed sequence of events. This process happens automatically and is completely free!

Immune system research is still in its infancy. The function of the thymus gland, which is the most important part of the immune system, was not discovered until 1961. Before this time it was thought to be a piece of redundant tissue similar to the appendix. Despite the fact that vaccinations have been used now for nearly one hundred years, no one really understands how the immune system responds to them.

Since the coming of AIDS (an immune deficient disease) research into how this system works has increased a hundredfold. The old theories as to how it works have not stood up to the test and are constantly changing as new information becomes available. We are in the midst of a radical, theoretical, revolution within the medical profession itself, with a vast number of books suddenly being written about the immune system. However, despite the ongoing re-evaluation of theories, some of the fundamental aspects of what causes this system to break down are being overlooked.

Firstly, the incidence of auto-immune diseases has risen dramatically in the last fifty years, during which time vaccinations have been available world-wide. These diseases include AIDS, rheumatoid arthritis, lupus erythematosus, candidias, MS (multiple sclerosis), ME (myalgic encephalomyelitis or post viral syndrome), and Guillain-Barre syndrome – all fairly new diseases of our modern world, and all related to an under- or over-active immune system. Yet no one seems to be looking at the possible relationship of the incidence of immune system diseases to the vaccination programmes.

Secondly, the mental and emotional health of the individual is extremely important. Very little recognition is given to the enormous influence that any emotional disturbance has on the immune system. The long and continued ill-effects of grief, loneliness, abuse of whatever nature, resentment, jealousy, anger, hatred, etc., are largely seen as having no relevance whatsoever to the physical body, as if our thoughts and feelings belonged to a separate life force. In fact these feelings and emotions are extremely relevant to the way the immune system works and can directly suppress its proper functioning. Anger and resentment affect the liver and gallbladder, grief affects the heart and lungs, fear affects the kidneys, stress affects the stomach, bowels, blood pressure and so on.

Alternative practitioners generally acknowledge the importance of mental and emotional symptoms when treating the whole person. For example, tonsillitis is often initially caused by an inability to express anger or tears, thereby creating an energy block in the throat. If this persists the poor flow of natural energy and blood will eventually create a susceptibility and infection will follow.

Very often acute infections are actually caused by stress or emotional trauma and it is always worth questioning if any event has upset the patient before the symptoms appeared. Commonly people, and of course children, will develop acute infections when there has been some traumatic event in their lives and this emotional condition must be taken into consideration. Sometimes an emotional remedy will clear the infection by removing the block to the immune system but if the infection is particularly severe it may have to be dealt with first and the emotional symptoms later.

Thirdly, the language used to describe the immune system is essentially violent, aggressive and defensive. In all the textbooks the role of the immune system is described in similar terms: it is likened to an army, trained and ready to defend the body against attack, to mount counter-attacks, and to arm it against possible future attack. Or its role is described as being similar to that of guard dogs or crime-prevention officers, well equipped with weapons designed to deal with the enemy – the germ! (Remember, the rats and flies come only where there is food for them to eat. They did not create the pile of rubbish upon which they feed.)

Nowhere in this type of language is there any understanding of the real role of the immune system: that is, to cleanse and re-balance a unit that is constantly having to deal with change. This aggressive and violent language reflects the essentially negative way in which we view ourselves and our society. The vaccination programme and the rationale behind it are part of the aggressive and paranoid way we view our world. To arm the young child against possible attack automatically puts him or her in a position of defence, causing a subtle, secondary mental state where they become wary, secretive, paranoid and aggressive to a greater or lesser degree according to their susceptibility.

Lastly, we should consider the importance of diet and exercise. As you will see in the next few paragraphs, the immune system is very dependent upon the movement of muscles to aid the flow of lymphatic fluid around the body. Regular exercise helps to keep this system clear of blockages and debris, and ensures various immune system cells move freely around the body as and where needed.

Diet is extremely important in that food provides the building blocks for all tissues. Food provides energy, enables thought processes to go on, enables every function of the body to continue and without it we would die. A healthy body needs clean, well prepared, uncontaminated foods of a great variety in order to maintain health and, the better one eats, the better everything will function.

HOW THE IMMUNE SYSTEM WORKS

Below is an overview of what the immune system consists of and how it works. It is made up of several main parts: the pituitary gland, the thymus gland, the lymphatic system, the bone marrow and the lymph nodes, spleen, appendix, tonsils and Peyer's Patches (see diagram).

The Pituitary Gland
This is found in the central brain and is the Director of Affairs. It liaises with all the other systems of the body and has the final say, so to speak, as to priorities of function.

The Thymus Gland
This is a small gland found just behind the breastbone. It is the central computer for the immune system and is responsible for programming all immune system cells and controlling the way they respond to their internal and external environment.

In the unborn child the thymus gland is responsible for programming all new cells with the body's *own* code. In future life, any cell with the "owner code" will not be rejected by its own immune system. This is very important. If this is not done properly it results in auto-immune diseases in later life, such as rheumatoid arthritis, juvenile diabetes, multiple sclerosis and, of course, AIDS,

The immune system itself is not fully developed until the age of six months. During this time the body is so designed that the mother's antibodies cover the child through breast-feeding until its own system is fully operational. The current vaccination programme begins at the ages of eight weeks, twelve weeks and sixteen weeks. The breast-fed child is better able to cope with such an onslaught when its immune computer is fully coded and functional.

The thymus gland is activated at birth by growth hormones and suppressed at puberty by sex hormones. It is therefore actively storing and gathering information in the first twelve years or so of life when the individual tests, examines and learns to deal effectively with the environment. This is when most of the immune system codes are formulated.

After puberty the thymus gland continues to control the immune system until death. However, what usually happens is that it slowly deteriorates, often becoming so damaged that its function is seriously undermined and severe illness follows. Autopsies done on older people in the past almost always revealed the thymus gland as a shrivelled and shrunken piece of tissue of unknown value found in the vicinity of the chest. This is why it has been viewed, along with the appendix (which is often found in the same condition), as a useless part of the anatomy, and why its importance was not recognised until the 1960s.

The Bone Marrow
Here, from birth to death, millions of blood cells are manufactured, including those that are directly concerned with the immune system. The most intense period of cell manufacture is from birth to puberty, after which time the process slows down.

The blood cells perform many different jobs. The red blood cells travel around the body in the blood stream. They consist of platelets (which help the blood to coagulate after injury) and erythrocytes (which mainly carry oxygen but also detect toxic material in the blood and inform other cells of its presence). White blood cells, or leucocytes, not only travel in the lymphatic fluid but also in the blood stream and where necessary they can infiltrate tissue itself. White blood cells are also sub-divided into polymorphs and monocytes.

Polymorphs have several jobs. They alert the immune system to damage, initiate inflammation, and then clear infection by ingesting and neutralising bacteria. Once this is done they usually die and become waste material or pus. This process is known as phagocytosis. Monocytes also use the process of phagocytosis to clear infection, but also play a major role in clearing debris generally from the blood, lymphatic system and tissues. They are bigger than polymorphs, there are fewer of them and, apart from acting as vacuum cleaners generally, they also manufacture many different enzymes and immune proteins that aid other cells to work properly.

The Lymphatic System
This is the network of blind channels that end in lymph nodes. These channels run alongside the blood vessels of the body and carry lymphatic fluid which contains the cells of the immune system. These cells are commonly known as white blood cells, polymorphs, lymphocytes and monocytes. Through this network, these cells are easily distributed anywhere in the body according to need and are responsible for clearing infection and debris for elimination.

Unlike the blood vessels, there is no pump (the heart) to move the lymphatic fluid around. The lymph channels run alongside the muscles and it is only by the action of muscles (or massage) that the lymphatic fluid is moved. This is why exercise is so important. Lack of exercise causes a build-up of waste material, with all its consequent problems, preventing the cells of the immune system from having easy access to all areas of the body.

The lymph nodes, found at the end of the lymph channels, are collection points for intense activity during illness or infection. This is why, when infection or illness occurs, these nodes (found in the neck, armpits and groin and throughout the body) swell up and become tender. It is a natural reaction of a healthy immune system and the nodes will return to normal when the system is cleared.

Lymph Nodes, Spleen, Appendix, Tonsils and Peyer's Patches
These areas produce other types of cells known as lymphocytes. Lymphocytes are quite sophisticated cells capable of memorising past infections. When an infection arises that has been known before, the lymphocytes rapidly

reproduce themselves and deal with it before it can take hold. They are further subdivided into T- and B-lymphocytes.

T-cells have all passed through the thymus gland at some stage for programming. T_H or T_4-cells (otherwise known as T-helper-cells) travel around the body and decide whether or not the immune system is needed to deal with a particular problem. They effectively switch on the immune system. T_S or T_8-cells (otherwise known as suppressor cells) switch off the immune system when the problem is over.

Cytotoxic T-cells are purely designed to look for viruses that are hidden within the cells of the body. They contain chemicals that actually break up the whole cell containing the virus, and the debris is then cleared by phagocytosis. Lymphokine-producing T-cells look for viruses that move between cells. They neutralise them with chemicals such as interferon and the debris is again cleared by phagocytosis.

B-lymphocytes deal more with bacteria or viruses that have been known before. The B-cells remove bacteria from the blood or lymph into the tissues and then ascertain their size and shape. They then make exact replicas of the bacteria, rapidly manufacturing them in their thousands, and take them back into the blood or lymph where they speedily attach themselves to the growing bacteria and neutralise them. Polymorphs then ingest the cells and clear the area. This process is known as antibody production.

The immune response: measles
There is very little information available as to immune system responses to measles or the measles vaccination. The only conclusion that can be drawn is that immune responses generally, and to vaccinations, are not yet fully understood.

More surprising is the fact that so little research has actually been done despite vaccinations being widely accepted for the past 100 years!

In 1988, so many children were falling seriously ill after having the MMR vaccination that a group of scientists, working from a well known London Hospital, decided to investigate.

They looked at 12 children between the ages of 3 and 10 years, all with similar symptoms – i.e. chronic enterocolitis (intestinal abnormalities including ulceration, nodule formation and severe pain, similar to Crohn's disease) and regressive developmental disorder (a type of autism). All the parents said that their children were developing normally in every respect before having the MMR. Various tests were conducted to try to discover the cause of these unusual and similar symptoms, and it was concluded that the only common denominator was the MMR vaccination.

One of the doctors conducting the trials advised that the vaccination should be withdrawn until it has been more fully tested. The Government denied any possible link and in fact proceeded to introduce the MMR booster to counteract the low uptake of this vaccination!

It is almost impossible to prove vaccine damage as the variables in day-to-day living are so great, but parents usually know what has upset their children and this was the only common factor. This investigation is on-going.

From the Homoeopathic point of view, it is very interesting to see these symptoms in their worst form. Similar symptoms appear in practice on a day-to-day basis. Side-effects of the MMR include anaemia, malabsorption, abdominal pain, bowel disorders, exhaustion, rashes and behavioural disturbances all to a greater or lesser degree according to the *susceptibility* of the individual.

One child from this group of unfortunate children was recently brought for homoeopathy and is described in Chapter 4. This clearly shows the susceptibility inherited from his family that would contraindicate any vaccination programme.

Statistics can, and often are, easily manipulated and vaccination damage is extremely difficult to prove. People cannot be fitted into graphs and statistics, the variables are too great. The main evidence of the damage caused by vaccinations is provided by observing wholly unvaccinated children and the effects of clearing the vaccinations. The differences speak for themselves. At the end of the day this type of evidence cannot be disputed.

As measles is such a topical disease, it would be interesting to take a look at how the immune system responds to it. Measles is a viral infection. Viruses are smaller than bacteria and can only reproduce inside the body's own cells. The virus then takes over the host cell. The measles virus first enters the body through the upper respiratory tract of the eyes, nose, throat or lungs, where it reproduces and rapidly spreads to local lymph nodes, causing swollen glands around the ears and neck. Histamine and other chemicals are released into the blood, causing a high temperature and dilation of blood vessels which attracts immune system cells to the infected area. Leucocytes and lymphocytes then go into action to clear the infection.

As the virus multiplies it is then shed into the blood, causing the second stage – the rash and the spread of the infection to other lymph nodes of the body. The temperature then comes down and after several more days the infection is finished. The disease lasts for about two weeks.

During this time the cells of the immune system will have been programmed to respond to future viral infections. Again, in the last fifty years viral infections have become much more prevalent and are extremely difficult to cure with orthodox medicine. It is very important to have an immune system that can deal effectively with viral infections. To suppress this ability in young children is a great mistake and leaves them much more vulnerable to viral infections in later life. If a child does have a mild dose of measles, the immune system generally is stretched, developed and programmed with new information that will help it deal with its environment in the future.

Historically, measles has been found in various parts of the world as a severe epidemic, often with many fatalities. As humanity evolved the immune system learned to deal with measles very effectively and the evolutionary process of working through many and varied infectious diseases has led to the complex and efficient immune system that we have today.

As people began to explore the world large masses of population who had not previously been exposed to measles were overcome by the infection and died. Eventually the population of those areas developed their own immunity. This has now happened world-wide and many thousands of people have died but, in doing so, the health and strength of the world population has increased and future generations are much stronger as a result.

To prolong a huge vaccination programme for a disease that has already been historically dealt with world-wide does not make sense and in fact is undermining the natural immunity built up by humanity over a long period of time. We should, instead, now be building upon the evolutionary work that has been done over the centuries.

The less chance a child has of getting a mild infection of this kind when the immune system is ready to learn and develop, the weaker the health of the individual becomes. With successive generations the immune system is getting weaker and weaker and less able to deal with the new epidemics we have to face, such as dangerous levels of toxins, radioactivity and pollution. These are all "man-made" and often invisible but present dangers in the food we eat, the air we breathe and the water we drink. We need an efficient, mature immune system to deal with this onslaught in order to survive the next hundred years while we attempt to clean up our devastated planet.

In practice, a well handled dose of measles promotes a positive development of the child. There is usually a growth spurt, more energy, a clearer mind and intellect and a general increase in the child's well-being. Obviously, if the individual child is particularly susceptible to that disease, then he or she will need help to get through it. Most children in this society get through measles without any medication at all.

With a natural infection of measles, a definite sequence of events takes place, and if the child is well looked after he or she recovers and benefits from the experience, despite its being rather intense. With vaccinations, the virus is injected directly into the muscle and causes a response only in the lymph nodes. Half of the natural immune system response is side-stepped and, if a temperature does occur, it is advised to suppress it with Calpol (children's paracetamol). Again, there is very little written on the chemical responses that take place, but certainly when the blood is tested after three weeks, antibodies to that disease will be found.

The dormant virus
It is now known that viruses can enter cells and lie dormant for many years. In later life, possibly triggered by stress or trauma, these hidden viruses may be reactivated and destroy the host cells in which they live. This is one theory as to why people develop auto-immune diseases such as cancer. To put a virus into the body through the back door, so to speak, must in some cases make it much easier for this to happen. Also, because the natural sequence of events has not been initiated, the immune system has to work harder to discover what is going on and easily becomes confused.

It would appear that to side-step the normal inflammatory response means that the virus is never properly synthesised, and the immune system poorly programmed, causing confusion and an immature ability to deal with viral infections of any kind in the future. Certainly, vaccinated children generally have less ability to deal with infections across the board and are prone to persistent viral infections. There are still many unanswered questions.

Anaphylactic Shock

Finally, it is important to look at another immune response to vaccinations known as "anaphylactic shock". This is a reaction to an injection of any foreign protein, such those found in the diphtheria and tetanus vaccinations and some types of insect stings. The first symptom is a swelling at the point of entry of the needle, usually from the first set of vaccinations. This is a warning to the doctor that the child is sensitive and could be allergic and the reaction should be noted. It is a warning sign of the possibility of anaphylactic shock with the next set of vaccinations. After the next vaccination the child may go into shock very suddenly with collapse, rapid breathing and low blood pressure. This may quickly lead to death unless the child is revived with an immediate injection of adrenaline or steroids.

CHAPTER THREE

MEASLES, MUMPS AND RUBELLA

The MMR is the latest vaccination to be introduced by the government in the UK, where it has been in general use for about ten years. It is given between the ages of twelve and eighteen months, as a triple injection, three diseases given in one. Because of this it is difficult to unravel the side-effects as they all overlap.

The mumps and measles part of the vaccine is cultured in chicken embryos and the rubella portion is cultured in lung tissue taken from a male foetus after termination of pregnancy from a mother who was mentally subnormal.

Two strains of this vaccination were withdrawn from general use because a high number of side-effects were reported. We are now assured that the new strains of the viruses are quite safe. All three are viral infections and it is viruses that can hide in cells and lie dormant for years, as discussed in Chapter Two.

In 1994 the medical profession decided that there might be a nasty epidemic of measles in the following year and that all children needed to be vaccinated against measles and rubella, whether they had already had the vaccination or not. This vaccination was called the MR (and it is interesting to note that most parents did not know their child was also being given a rubella vaccination). The effectiveness of the MMR given at fifteen months had been very poor and the medical profession felt children were still "at risk". Although measles does come in cycles and can be reasonably predicted, to vaccinate not just with measles but also rubella on top of the fifteen other vaccinations the child will already have had is a totally unnecessary overload of the immune system.

In 1997 there was an outcry from parents and doctors who were experiencing severe reactions to the "safe" MMR vaccination. Many children were exhibiting signs and symptoms similar to Crohn's disease and autism (more fully described in Chapter 2). Some of these children were so badly damaged that trials were started at a London hospital and doctors there advised that this vaccination be withdrawn until more tests were done and the vaccination proved to be safe.

The reaction from the government to this was not, as might have been expected, to withdraw the vaccination until further trials had been carried out, but to introduce the MMR booster to ensure that every child had the vaccination. This means that children could now possibly have had the original MMR vaccination plus the MR booster and the new MMR booster as well, despite the advice given by the medical profession itself.

After hearing this, a lot of parents did not want to do this vaccination at all, and the booster was introduced to ensure its full uptake and catch any children that may have previously slipped throughout the MMR net. Many parents also wanted to have this vaccination done in three separate lots, but they were discouraged from having this choice on financial grounds.

There is currently a legal battle going on to obtain compensation for the damage that this vaccination has done to some children, backed by the help of an organisation called "Vaccine Victim Support" (details at the back of the book).

When one takes a historical look at vaccine damage over the last one hundred years, one sees that this situation has happened many times before. A new vaccine is introduced, despite it not being fully tested, and proves to be unstable and dangerous. Many children suffer damage to a greater or lesser degree but governments cover up the issue and continue to use it. Behind the scenes many doctors and scientists then frantically try to find out what is going on and eventually iron out instabilities and produce a fresh batch of a "better strain of vaccine".

For example, the polio vaccine has been through many changes since its introduction. Many children were severely damaged and some died in the process. Millions of pounds and dollars were paid out in compensation and now, 50 years on, this vaccine is relatively safe, although there are still side-effects and dangers according to the susceptibility of the individual. Exactly the same thing has happened with all the vaccines. France recently stopped using the hepatitis vaccine as it was causing neurological damage. Why does this happen in reverse? Any other drug has to be tested to its extreme before it is given a licence for general sale, but vaccinations seem to have some magical licence all of their own and are allowed to be tested on the general public instead of in the laboratory.

One of the children currently undergoing examination by the aforementioned London hospital has been brought for Homoeopathy. His case is described further on in this chapter and shows the worst scenario. The case is still being dealt with.

Measles

Measles is an air-borne, viral infection that passes from one child to another by coughing and sneezing. The disease begins with fever, a temperature of up to 39.5°C, a watery, runny nose, sneezing, conjunctivitis, laryngitis, a hoarse voice, mild cough, and possibly an intolerance to light (photophobia). This is known as the catarrhal stage and is very similar to the common cold. Prior to the appearance of the rash, the only symptom that distinguishes measles from the common cold is a mild inflammation of the mucous membranes in the mouth, known as Koplik's Spots. If you look in the mouth you will see small white spots surrounded by a red ring of inflammation on the mucous membrane.

The second, or exanthematous stage starts around the fourth day when a rash appears behind the ears and on the forehead, spreading to the face and body within hours. The rash consists of small spots that fuse together to form large blotchy areas, and is usually accompanied by crying and irritability. The child is infectious for fourteen days from the appearance of the rash and should be kept quietly at home.

There are several complications that can occur with measles which are listed below. The majority of children only get the milder symptoms but, if a child is susceptible, the more severe complications may arise. Again, the susceptibility of the individual is most important. While reading the list of complications, remember that what a disease can do to a susceptible child the vaccinations can also do.

Complications

1. Stomatitis – inflammation of the mouth which is seen as cracks or sores in the corners of the lips. This can cause a secondary infection of the parotid glands known as suppurative parotitis.

2. Croup, laryngitis and bronchitis.

3. Convulsions (fits) due to fever.

4. Acute suppurative otitis media (inflammation of the middle ear) caused by secondary infection. The symptoms are the same as for any acute ear

infection: severe pain, crying and holding or pulling the affected ear.

5. Corneal ulceration from severe conjunctivitis.

6. Bronchiolitis (inflammation of the tubes in the lungs). Bronchiectasis (dilation of the tubes in the lungs). The latter can follow bronchiolitis and has its own set of symptoms and complications, such as lung abscesses, empyema (a collection of pus in a lung cavity), broncho-pneumonia, pericarditis (inflammation of the muscle of the heart), septicaemia (which may cause an abscess anywhere in the body, including the brain) and finally, amyloidosis. This is a slow degeneration of tissue caused by long-term infection anywhere in the body and gives a lardy appearance to the tissues of the heart, spleen, kidneys and liver.

7. Broncho-pneumonia, another secondary infection which, if it overcomes the system, can be fatal.

8. Acute encephalitis. This is an inflammation of the brain, accompanied by headache, pyrexia (high temperature), restlessness and drowsiness. It is interesting to note that most medical text books list the causes of encephalitis as various viral infections such as measles, chickenpox, influenza, rabies and the measles vaccination. Recovery may be complete or partial. In rare cases encephalitis is fatal.

One rarely sees the last three complications of the above list and certainly no competent physician would allow an infection of this nature to go so far. However they do happen, both naturally and from the vaccination.

Some useful remedies that can be used during an infection of measles are listed below. It is always best to seek professional advice, especially if the child is particularly ill, but any of the following appropriate homoeopathic remedies, used in low doses, can be extremely helpful in getting the child through without too much distress.

Useful homoeopathic remedies for measles:-

1. Aconite – for use where the child is anxious and restless, has bloodshot eyes, a high fever, a dry, barking cough and a rough, itching or burning rash.

2. Belladonna – bright red rash, high fever without sweat, flushed face, glassy eyes and semi-delirious state.

3. Euphrasia – streaming, burning eyes, dislike of bright light, dry cough, rash, lots of sneezing and bland discharge from eyes and nose.

4. Gelsemium – hot and cold shivers, sneezing, sore throat, heavy headache with pain at the back of the head, face dark red and the child is drowsy and lethargic.

5. Pulsatilla – mild fever, dry mouth but not thirsty, the child is hot and wants fresh air, is weepy and clingy and has lots of yellow catarrh from eyes and nose. This remedy is the main one for mild measles and covers most cases.

In the UK measles is not a serious disease. Most parents today find it quite difficult to understand why they have to have their child vaccinated against this particular disease when their mothers used to organise measles parties to ensure all the children of the family had it. In fact a mild dose of measles stimulates the immature immune system, in the correct sequence, to develop naturally thereby strengthening the child generally. It also helps the immune system to deal generally with viruses. Most children have a growth spurt and become more mature mentally after a dose of measles.

From observations of children in practice the vaccination, apart from possibly causing any or all of the above "complications" according to the individual's susceptibility, also suppresses this natural development of the immune system and causes a dullness of the intellect and a lowering of energy and vitality. When unvaccinated children have contracted the disease and been given the appropriate remedies they recover well and are usually in better health than before.

As was mentioned in Chapter Two on the immune system, measles was responsible for wiping out vast numbers of people of all ages world wide. We now have a certain amount of immunity built in as a result of the natural evolutionary process, and no vaccination can take the place of this historical immunity. In fact, the measles vaccination is possibly reversing the progress achieved by reintroducing the disease and suppressing the immune system. This particular disease, historically, was almost extinct.

Mumps

Mumps, another air-borne disease, can also be contracted by contact, i.e. kissing. It is a viral infection of the salivary glands and usually affects young adults and school children.

The symptoms appear eighteen days after the initial infection and include loss of appetite (anorexia), nausea, painful swelling of either or both of the parotid glands and possible swelling of the salivary glands (under the chin). The patient should be isolated for fourteen days from the start of the swelling and be quietly rested in bed. The mouth is often dry and chewing is painful, so a nutritious semi-liquid diet may be necessary.

Complications

1. Orchitis in boys or oöphoritis in girls, where the disease has spread to other glands, in this case gonads or the ovaries. Usually only one side is affected, becoming swollen and tender, and may later atrophy (waste away), possibly causing infertility in later life.

2. Pancreatitis, inflammation of the pancreas. (This organ is responsible for the production of insulin and damage can lead to diabetes.) Symptoms include nausea, vomiting, pain and tenderness in the upper stomach.

3. Acute lymphocytic meningitis, or inflammation of the meninges of the brain, causing headache, fever and intolerance to light.

4. Encephalomyelitis. Symptoms are fever, intolerance of light, headache and drowsiness. This is an inflammation of the myelin sheath in the upper spine. The myelin sheath protects the spinal cord and damage to it causes multiple sclerosis.

Again it is rare to see the more serious complications of this disease and most cases clear up without any long-lasting effects. In 15 years of practice I have only seen one case of mumps and that was in a child whose mother had recently been killed in a road accident. The shock caused him to become susceptible. His mumps responded beautifully to homoeopathic Belladonna and he was back on his feet within a few days.

Useful homoeopathic remedies for mumps:

1. Belladonna – the child is semi-delirious, has a high fever without sweat,

plus inflammation of the right parotid gland.

2. Lachesis – large swelling and inflammation of the left parotid gland, very painful, and the child does not want to be touched, is hot, wants fresh air, has a bad sore throat and is irritable.

3. Mercurius solibulis – mainly the right side affected, extreme thirst and fever with sweating, foul breath and tongue, and the child is restless.

4. Phytolacca – inflammation and swelling of both parotid glands which feel stony hard to touch, sore throat and shooting pains up into the ears.

Rubella

Rubella, or German measles, is another air-borne disease spread from child to child by sneezing and coughing. It more commonly affects children over six years old and young adults. It appears two to three weeks after the initial infection and begins with fever, malaise, mild conjunctivitis, sore throat and aching joints.

The rash begins behind the ears, spreads to the forehead and face and then down the body. It appears as a flat, pink rash that lasts three to four days only, then the skin dries up and it flakes off. Lymph nodes at the back of the neck become swollen and tender causing stiffness. It is an extremely mild disease lasting only a few days, but complications may arise in susceptible children.

Complications

1. Polyarthralgia, painful joints similar in nature to rheumatoid arthritis (an auto-immune disease).

2. Thrombocytopenic purpura, tiny haemorrhages on the skin that disappear completely when the platelet count in the blood returns to normal.

3. Encephalomyelitis. an inflammation of the myelin sheath that protects the spinal cord (described under the complications of mumps).

4. Infection during the first three months of pregnancy may cause malformation of the brain, heart, eyes or ears of the unborn foetus.

The fourth complication is serious and I can well understand the theory behind this particular vaccination. The prospect of a child being maimed in this way is horrific and, for the parents of such a child, must be unbearable. However, the evolutionary process of developing immunity cannot be simulated through vaccination. Another way is to strengthen the mother and test her susceptibility before conception so that should she come into contact with Rubella in the early months of pregnancy, she would be able to deal with the infection without it becoming a serious problem. Many children still get rubella despite being vaccinated, but are then left undiagnosed. This in turn puts many people at risk and creates general confusion.

Useful homoeopathic remedies for rubella:-

1. Aconite – fever with sweat, chills and restlessness. Thirst, sore throat and anxiety. Useful remedy in the first stages of rubella and often all that is needed.

2. Ferrum phosphoricum – this covers most mild cases where the fever is lower, symptoms similar to Aconite but very mild.

3. Gelsemium – this is useful where the child is more languid than restless, has no energy and little thirst. It will help the rash to come out.

Generally german measles is such a mild disease, in most children, that no treatment is needed at all.

Stephen – born June 1990
This eight-year-old came to see me for homoeopathy in September 1998 suffering from "Persistent Measles Virus Disease" diagnosed by doctors at a London hospital where he is under treatment and investigation.

He has no speech, has had severe pain in his abdomen for many years, constantly walks up and down on tip-toes and has all the signs and symptoms of autism and severe enteritis, which is similar in nature to Crohn's disease. The only thing that has helped him so far is Repleat and vitamin B_{12} injections that he has on a regular basis. This child has so many complicated symptoms it is hard to know where to start and it is very difficult to see clearly what has caused what.

At three days old he was given the BCG vaccination plus a vitamin K injection. Then the regular DPT and Polio, but not Hib. At 15 months he was also given a typhoid vaccination, although no-one knows why.

Shortly before having the MMR at 15 months, Stephen had a normal bout of German measles and his mother, at the time, questioned why he had to have the MMR when he had already had one of the diseases and was therefore immune to it. She was told this did not matter and to go ahead. In her opinion the MMR was an overload of an immune system that was still dealing with the after-effects of the rubella infection and that he had a high level of that antibody still in his system. She feels that this also contributed to his susceptibility and was the main cause of Stephen's problems. She would have preferred to have given him only the Mumps and Measles vaccination without the Rubella portion.

Two months after the MMR vaccination he began to go downhill with repeated ear infections, diarrhoea, lethargy, weak muscles, excessive wind, strong smelling urine and would sleep with his thumbs jammed in his ears.

By the time he was two years old, his speech had deteriorated and he began to do strange things like walking on his toes, lying on the floor screaming, seemingly in pain, and head-banging. He was eventually diagnosed as autistic and was given further tests to find out what was wrong with him physically. After many tests (including a lumbar puncture) they discovered he was B_{12} deficient.

Two years ago, at age six, he was referred to a London hospital where they did more tests, including an MRI scan and an endoscopy, and discovered ulceration of the bowel which had been causing him extreme pain. His parents have found that simple Repleat helps him enormously with the pain in his abdomen and B_{12} injections and other vitamins have helped him generally.

He is caught in a daily cycle that looks like his immune system is stuck in measles symptoms, hence the diagnosis "Persistent Measles Virus Disease". Every day he gets hot and dry, becomes irritable and weepy, goes bright red with a high temperature, and develops a rash behind his ears and on his cheeks. It all lasts about ten minutes and quickly dies down again.

His family history is very interesting and shows that Stephen was ripe for vaccine damage due to the genetic weakness of his family, in particular in the digestive sphere.

His mother has five sisters and two brothers, all of whom have had stomach problems, mainly pernicious anaemia and ulcers. His mother had mild pernicious anaemia before he was born, her older sister has severe pernicious anaemia and has to have blood transfusions every six months, one sister also had double measles and now suffers from MS, two sisters and both brothers all suffer from stomach ulcers, his mother's father also had stomach ulcers, and there is lots of cancer in the grandparents on both sides. This should be enough for any doctor to decide to leave well alone and not overload the immune system with vaccinations. However, it was not well left and Stephen, like many others, has had to pay the price. So far, Stephen has not responded to the initial clear-out by homoeopathic remedies, other than a lessening of the measles-type fever and rash he was getting on a daily basis. It would seem that part of the problem has been caused by the mercury added to the MMR and I am currently working along these lines.

With such severe cases, simply clearing the vaccines with remedies is not enough. Neurological damage is almost impossible to cure and the best one can do in such a situation is to bring the child into as good health as possible. Specialists at the London hospital are also working to find ways to undo the damage done, and are sincerely and honestly looking at the truth of the matter, even though their findings are being ignored by the majority of medical and government officials.

Rose – born December 1991
This baby was brought to me in March 1993. She was fourteen months old with an eczematous rash that she had had for four months, since the previous October. The rash was all over her body, worse in the creases of her arms and legs, and looked like a mass of little red spots. It was extremely itchy, especially when she was tired.

She had initially been diagnosed with urticaria, for which she was prescribed anti-histamine syrup. When this did not work it was re-diagnosed as eczema and she was prescribed hydrocortisone ointment, Oilatum and paraffin. All of these helped a little, but the rash persisted.

Rose was fairly healthy otherwise; she slept well, but was bad tempered, clingy and stubborn. On looking carefully at the case there did not seem to be any apparent cause for the rash. She had had all the recommended vaccinations, including the MMR, and as the rash looked so much like measles, I decided to give her first a homoeopathic remedy made from the

MMR in the 30th potency to see if the vaccination had caused her condition or was blocking her natural development. That night her throat swelled up, just as if she had mumps, and she was hot and irritable. The next morning the swelling had gone down and she was much happier. Over the next week the rash slowly disappeared from the top downwards.

Three weeks later I saw her again and the rash had almost completely gone, there was just a little left on her ankles. The vaccination had only partially activated the immune system and again caused "Persistent Measles Virus disease". The remedy gave the body that extra stimulus to clear itself and deal with the disease onslaught effectively. The rash has not returned and she now has a lovely peaches-and-cream complexion.

I saw Rose again in May 1995 for restless sleep and temper tantrums, but she still has her peaches and cream complexion and is physically very well.

Barnaby – born December 1992
This small boy was brought to me in July 1994. He had persistent, recurring ear infections since the age of three months. He had already had many courses of antibiotics and was due to have grommets put in his ears in the near future. (Grommets are small rubber rings inserted through the ear drum, under general anaesthetic, to provide a drain for the mucus that collects in the inner ear).

He was difficult from birth and did not sleep. He also had slight eczema from birth that had worsened after the first lot of vaccinations at two months. He was given cortisone which cleared the eczema.

On the night after the first two sets of vaccinations he became irritable, developed a high temperature and started projectile vomiting. The doctor recommended Calpol (infant paracetamol) and the symptoms subsided. There was no reaction to the third set of vaccinations.

He occasionally suffered from hives (an allergic reaction), was a little hyperactive, had had diarrhoea for the last six weeks and was generally very "whingey". He panted as he breathed, was slightly wheezy, was always mouth-breathing and had a constantly blocked nose. The family history was not clear, but his mother had had repeated ear infections and there was hay fever in his father's family.

Barnaby seemed to me to be suffering the many and varied side-effects of the vaccinations (homoeopathically termed "vaccinosis"). No serious pathology, but general discomfort and lowered vitality. The first thing to do was to clear the picture and see what was happening by giving him homoeopathic doses of MMR, DPT and Polio in the 200th potency and Hib in the 30th potency.

From the first dose of the MMR 200, within twenty four hours the change was dramatic. His diarrhoea disappeared, he slept well, ate well, and was no longer hyperactive. Soon after he developed mild chicken pox, was covered in spots, but not ill in himself and made a full recovery.

Eight weeks after his initial appointment with me he had another visit to the hospital to have his ears checked and possibly to have grommets inserted. He was examined thoroughly and his ears were found to be completely clear, except for some slight pink scarring from previous infections. His hearing was perfect. I advised a dairy-free diet and gave him his constitutional remedy, which was much easier to see since clearing the vaccinations. He is now extremely well and full of life.

Atlanta – born November 1992
Atlanta was brought to me in February 1994 with persistent ear infections and patches of dry skin. There were no apparent reactions to the vaccinations but she had her first ear infection at six months and again in January 1994, shortly after the MMR vaccination. She was given antibiotics both times and her mother was worried that this would continue and that she might end up with serious ear problems.

Atlanta was basically happy and well, a very good eater although excessively thirsty, and a good sleeper although she slept in the classic catarrhal position, on her face with her bottom in the air.

I gave her the standard homoeopathic remedies to clear the side-effects of the vaccinations and saw her again a month later, at which time she was completely better. She had no problems with her ears, her skin had cleared, and her thirst was normal. I did not give her any remedy other than the vaccination ones. I heard from Atlanta's mother again in August 1995, and she had not had any ear infections at all and had been very well, except for the dry skin that had returned after some months but which was not serious.

Jemima – born August 1996

Jemima came to me for treatment in September 1998 with general malaise. She was extremely thin, pale, did not want anyone to come near her despite coming from an obviously loving and nurturing family. She had a very poor appetite, some days would not eat anything but was always extremely thirsty. On examination I found her mouth was full of a white coating that could only be thrush. She also suffered from painful stools that were often hard and light in colour, had lots of abdominal wind and bad breath.

She slept fairly well but always woke at 5am and after her afternoon nap would wake screaming and screaming. She also had a permanent cold for the last three months and would sometimes cough until she vomited and would then throw up lots of clear mucus.

On the positive side, she was also full of energy most of the time, very bright and intelligent, loving and talkative once she got to know people and very much a child who knew her own mind.

From birth she had had a very difficult time. Her birth was not easy as she was in the wrong position, came out bottom first and had to be revived for an hour after. The next day they found a small hole in her heart but this has not been a problem. She was then okay and was breast fed for 6 months despite her mother having repeated mastitis that was treated with antibiotics.

Two weeks after the first lot of vaccinations she developed bronchiolitis and ended up in hospital. After that she got a chest or ear infection every few weeks and had antibiotics each time. She had had at least 20 courses of antibiotics to date, hence the thrush.

She also, during that time, developed a patch of herpes on her genital area.

This case presented a lot of mixed up symptoms so, as usual, I first of all gave her the vaccination clear-out in order to find out what was causing what.

From the first remedy, the MMR 200, she began to throw off green mucus from her eyes and nose, stopped drinking altogether and was foul tempered. Her mother took her to the hospital, where the doctors could not understand what was happening and sent her away, but on her next visit to the Osteopathic Children's Centre (where they also do a lot of work around vaccine damage) they advised her to stop all dairy products, which she did.

There was a big reaction to each of the remedies after that. After the DPT 200 she had excessive urination, poured green mucus from one nostril and was again foul tempered. All these symptoms were short-lived and she soon began to pick up.

I saw her again in December and there had been a tremendous improvement. She was eating like a horse, had put on weight, had grown in height, was sleeping through to 7am, and was generally much happier.

I am still seeing Jemima on a regular basis and she has grown from strength to strength. She has not had a single infection since coming and needed no antibiotics. However, her herpes persists, showing this was nothing to do with the vaccinations, it is a separate issue that has to be dealt with accordingly. All her other symptoms abated after having the side-effects of the vaccinations cleared.

CHAPTER FOUR

DIPHTHERIA, PERTUSSIS AND TETANUS

Like the MMR, this vaccination is three in one. It is given first at the age of eight weeks, by injection into the arm or thigh, then again at twelve weeks and sixteen weeks. It is further recommended that the diphtheria and tetanus be given again as a pre-school booster between three and five years old. Tetanus is given again to school leavers and recommended every ten years thereafter.

This is another triple vaccination, bound together with aluminium compounds. It is difficult to unravel the side-effects, as they overlap. Below is an account of each individual disease with its possible complications and some more case histories from my own practice.

Diphtheria

This is an air-borne bacterial infection, but it can also be contracted through direct contact with fomites (infected objects such as blankets or clothes, that may harbour bacteria). Symptoms appear two to four days from initial infection and the throat becomes sore and covered with a pearly-grey, raised and very sticky membrane surrounded by inflammation. Lymph nodes in the neck swell and become tender, the larynx narrows, causing noisy breathing, the voice becomes husky and the breath foul smelling. The diphtheria bacteria localise in the throat but produce toxins that enter the general system, causing apathy, headache, mild fever, protein in the urine and possibly a red rash. If the membrane covering the throat is removed, the surface bleeds.

Complications

1. Acute toxic myocarditis: this affects the muscle of the heart, causing a rapid but weak pulse, low blood pressure and pallor, and can be fatal by causing heart failure.

2. Respiratory obstruction by the membrane itself, causing breathlessness and cyanosis (blueness of the skin and lips from lack of oxygen). Treatment is by tracheostomy (opening the throat surgically and inserting a breathing tube). The membrane may also be inhaled, causing pulmonary collapse and possibly broncho-pneumonia.

3. Neurological damage due to the toxins from the bacteria entering the nervous system. It begins with paralysis of the soft palate, with a nasal

voice and fluids coming up through the nose on swallowing. By the fourth week the eye muscles are involved and if the disease progresses further, paralysis of the diaphragm occurs, causing respiratory failure and polyneuritis (inflammation of peripheral nerves).

If the patient survives all these complications a total recovery is made.

Undoubtedly this disease is nasty, even in its minor state, but once again we must be aware that a susceptible individual is also susceptible to the side-effects of the vaccination.

Diphtheria is very rare these days in our society. In practice there are many small children suffering with low-grade but persistent symptoms similar to mild diphtheria: apathy, swollen glands, croaky voice and persistent sore throats, leading sometimes to tonsillectomy. But again it is difficult to prove that this is vaccine damage until the vaccine is cleared and the child reverts to good health. Then one can see that it was the vaccine that set up the chronic condition.

The medical profession states that this disease has been eradicated wholly by the vaccination programme. A closer look reveals that these programmes were set up as the disease was already in decline. Indeed, diphtheria was declining by 1920 and the main vaccination programme was set up in 1940. When a disease is naturally in decline, the vaccination programme actually increases the incidence of it – and there are many well-recorded incidents of outbreaks of this disease in wholly vaccinated communities!

Useful Homeopathic remedies for Diptheria

1. Apis – the throat is bright red, puffy and looks varnished, the child is hot, irritable and cannot bear anything to touch the throat.

2. Arsenicum Album – the child is restless, weak and chilly, extremely thirsty but only sips fluids and the throat looks dry and shrivelled.

3. Lac Caninum – the child is nervous and sensitive, the throat looks pearly white and the pain moves from side to side.

4. Lachesis – the child seems talkative and irritable, feels hot and wants fresh air. The throat membrane starts on the left and moves to the right and has

a blue appearance. The child complains of a choking feeling and does not want the throat to be touched.

5. Mercurius – this can affect one or both sides of the throat which has a thick yellow or white membrane covering it. The child is hot, thirsty, sweaty and restless, with foul breath.

Pertussis
Commonly known as whooping cough, this is the most documented of all the vaccinations and the most controversial (until the recent MMR). Historically, whooping cough was a deadly and highly infectious disease which ravaged large communities throughout the world. In Europe, its virility began to decline from the mid-18th century onwards, due to the evolution of natural immunity and the beginnings of proper community sanitation and care.

As with all infectious diseases, poor sanitation, deficient nutrition and general poverty lay the foundations for mass susceptibility, and as these conditions have improved, the strength of the disease has diminished. Even today the worst cases of whooping cough are still seen where there is a poor standard of living.

The vaccination was introduced in 1912 by two French doctors and immunisation began in earnest in the 1930s. Side-effects of this vaccination began to emerge soon after its introduction, and it has been the source of much wrangling and debate within the medical profession ever since. One medical doctor even stated that the neurological damage done to children who had had the disease was less than the damage done to the unfortunate victims of the vaccinations.

The side-effects of this vaccination are well recorded and a lot has been written about it. Controversy has not only prevailed among alternative practitioners but also within the orthodox medical profession itself. The best sources of information on the subject are several books written by Harrison Coulter, an American historian. He researched the terrible effects of this vaccination over twenty years in the USA, where the vaccination is compulsory. His findings are extremely well documented and well worth reading.

It is important to remember that a susceptible child will automatically be susceptible to the side-effects of the vaccination. Any child who exhibits a severe reaction to the vaccination would probably also succumb to the disease itself, but at least then that child would have a chance of strengthening his or her immune system with the help of good treatment, nutrition and care.

Homoeopathy excels in this type of work, but it is necessary to have the courage to work with this system of medicine and the practitioner must be prepared to work hard to obtain the desired results.

Useful Homoeopathic remedies for Pertussis:

1. Belladonna – High fever with no sweat, red face and glassy eyes. Very specific cough – the child feels much better for coughing up even a little mucus but soon after the lungs get dryer and dryer and start to tickle then spasm, gagging, vomiting and the well known "whoop".

2. Coccus Cacti – Fits of coughing that end in vomiting strings of clear or white mucus. Attacks are worse at night, can be prevented by drinks of cold water and the child is hot and wants to lie without any bed clothes on.

3. Drosera – Coughing follows itself so rapidly the child can hardly draw breath. The cough is also very painful and tickly and the child holds its diaphragm to prevent the pain. The cough is worse at night and the child irritable and angry.

4. Kali Carbonicum – Dry, hard, raking rough, worse at night, especially at 3am, with vomiting; the child has puffy eyelids, is cold and sweaty.

Whooping cough is another air-borne bacillus, *Bordatella pertussis,* spread from one child to another by coughing and sneezing. The droplets enter the body through the mucous membranes of the nose, throat and lungs. It occurs mainly in children under five years old and is most dangerous in small babies.

Seven to fourteen days after initial infection, symptoms appear similar to those of the common cold: conjunctivitis, sneezing, runny nose and cough. This is known as the catarrhal stage.

Over the next two to four weeks the cough gets worse and comes in short, sharp attacks of up to twenty coughs at a time, ending in the child coughing up thick, stringy white mucus followed by a deep inhalation of air through narrowed vocal chords that sounds like a "whoop". This is usually accompanied by vomiting. This is known as the paroxysmal stage. Each time the child coughs the tongue is scraped over the bottom teeth causing a painful ulcer and adding to the general misery of child and parent.

Complications

1. Broncho-pneumonia due to weakened lungs becoming susceptible to other organisms.

2. Atelectasis (lung collapse) caused by mucus obstructing the bronchi.

3. Bronchiectasis, which may follow atelectasis, is an abnormal dilatation of the bronchi, causing an accumulation of mucus that cannot be coughed up and which becomes chronically infected.

4. Convulsions caused by lack of oxygen to the brain during a severe fit of coughing.

5. Nose bleeds or haemorrhage in the eyes caused by venous congestion in the head.

6. Umbilical hernia or rectal hernia caused by undue pressure in the abdomen when coughing.

Reactions to watch for after the vaccination are, first, a swelling at the point of injection followed by fever. In most cases this is mild, and the child soon reverts to normal. If the swelling and fever are severe, this should be reported to the GP and would contraindicate further use of the vaccine.

There are many well documented cases of the fever rising as high as 105°F (40.5C), accompanied by a high-pitched wailing, known as "cri encéphalique" which may continue for hours, days or weeks. The baby goes deathly white, seems to pass out, turns blue and breathes shallowly. All this is very frightening and can be fatal.

All these side-effects should be notified to the doctor, but most busy GPs simply advise the use of Calpol to control the fever. Many parents have experienced the trauma of such side-effects, happily of short duration, however they have never been advised not to re-vaccinate their child in the future.

Tetanus

This is indeed a controversial disease, filling people with fear and dread, and parents really struggle when deciding whether or not to vaccinate their child against it. "But what if....?" is the cry that goes up whenever this subject is broached. It is the most maligned and misunderstood of all the infectious diseases and the terror that is put into people's hearts and minds concerning its effects are out of proportion to the actual threat that it poses.

The Tetanus bacterium, Clostridium Tetani, lives harmlessly in the intestines, mainly of horses, but also of some farm animals and some humans. It is excreted through the faeces of the carrier and can lie dormant for many years in soil in the form of spores.

If these spores enter a wound and become embedded in damaged tissue, and if there is no oxygen present, they may re-activate and become vegetable bacilli. This in itself is harmless and remains localised, but the bacilli may give off a neurotoxin that enters the blood stream and damages the central nervous system. Tetanus cannot live in oxygen, so the wound has to be deep or dirty in order for the bacilli to get a hold. Then the conditions have to be exactly right for this to happen and many wounds contain the spores with no untoward reaction. It is a rare disease in this modern age in which cars have taken over from horses and we no longer throw our excreta out onto the street!

In Europe, during the Victorian era, horses were the main system of transport and horse manure was everywhere. It was easy for a child to fall over in the street, cut him or herself, and not bother to wash the wound. At that time there was no clean running water and people were not aware of the benefits of washing. The Victorians eventually realised the disastrous results of an unhygienic environment and began to build sewers and drains and to educate people on the benefits of cleanliness and hygiene. Good for them, but are we still living in the early 1900s or are we now entering the 21st century with all *its* problems and diseases that need to be resolved?

Complications

The disease itself comes from a bacterium called *Clostridium tetani,* which enters the bloodstream through wounds. It is not infectious in the same way as the other diseases and cannot be caught from another person. If there is no oxygen present, the bacterium will change into a bacillus that produces a neurotoxin which can enter the blood stream and affects the nervous system. Symptoms appear from between two to twenty-one days after the wound has occurred. Early signs are stiffness of the muscles close to the wound, followed by stiffness of the jaw muscles and an inability to open the mouth properly. As the disease progresses the jaw muscles go into spasm, causing lockjaw, or trismus, and the muscles pull the lips away from the teeth, causing the well known fixed smile, *risus sardonicus*. Muscles of the neck, head, back, chest and extremities become rigid, pulling the body either forwards or backwards. Accompanying these symptoms are convulsive seizures which can be brought on by the slightest stimulus, such as a draught or loud noises.

As the bacilli toxins affect the central nervous system, it becomes sensitive and easily overstimulated and the seizures are extreme and very distressing. These symptoms are also accompanied by profuse sweating and sometimes high fever, but not always, and in a strong individual the disease will then begin to abate over the next few days and a full recovery is made. However, where there is a weakness of the nervous system and the disease takes over, death occurs mainly from asphyxia after prolonged spasms of the lungs.

As with all the other diseases, where there is a susceptibility to the disease there is also a susceptibility to the vaccination, and one can see here the possibility of an over-stimulated nervous system, a tendency to convulsions and constriction of the lung muscles. The similarities between the symptoms of this disease and certain types of asthma cannot be ignored.

There are two types of tetanus innoculations. First, the absorbed vaccine. This is made from the neurotoxin produced by the activated bacilli, treated with a disinfectant (formaldehyde), and prepared with aluminium hydroxide or aluminium phosphate. This is the one that is given in the DPT.

The second is human anti-tetanus immunoglobulin. This is made from human blood serum that has a high ratio of tetanus antibodies from recent infection or recent immunisation. This gives a direct boost to the antibodies in the blood and is used at the time of infection from a wound in people who have not previously been vaccinated against tetanus.

Tetanus is not like other infectious diseases. It is the direct result of mechanical injury and of foreign material entering the body. However, the question of susceptibility is still relevant.

Tetanus and homoeopathic first aid

Homoeopathy has been used for first aid in all sorts of situations over the last two hundred and fifty years. One famous doctor, Dr Dorothy Shepherd, used it at the front in World War I, with much better results than her colleagues who did not. Her book, *Homoeopathy and First Aid* (published by C.W. Daniel & Co., Ltd) is well worth reading and gives easy guidelines for using homoeopathy in first aid situations.

There are two main remedies for use in such a situation. First, Hypericum, or St John's Wort. This can be used internally as a remedy, and externally as a herbal cleansing wash. It is used for damage to nerves and specifically for torn or lacerated wounds (where there is the possibility of tetanus spores being present). The remedy, given at least in the 200th potency, relieves the pain and shock and has an extremely beneficial effect on the nervous system.

I once badly tore the skin on the back of my hand while gardening. The wound was very messy and dirty, and removing the dirt would have meant removing some portions of skin, which I could not bring myself to do. I washed it as best I could and took some homoeopathic Hypericum in the 200th potency. Within seconds the pain and shock were relieved, and the wound itself healed completely within five days. I continued to take the Hypericum for those five days, two a day, and made a full and pain-free recovery.

Also, when I was a student of homoeopathy, I severed the top of my finger in my car engine! Luckily I was wearing leather gloves, and these saved it being too mangled and dirty. I fainted and soon after was taken to casualty. The wound was very clean (and very painful) but, routinely, I was offered a tetanus shot. When I refused I was hauled before the sister in charge and given a lecture on responsibility. I still refused and never went back to the hospital. I have never had a tetanus vaccination myself and have treated myself purely with homoeopathy. This was when I discovered that homoeopathy works – and works gently.

The second remedy is Ledum. This is a herb called Marsh Tea which, when made into a homoeopathic remedy, is specific for puncture wounds of any type. It again relieves the pain and shock quickly and gently and helps heal the wound.

I was in a friend's garden a couple of years ago when her young daughter came running in with a rusty rake hanging out of her leg. She had fallen off her swing onto a rake that was hidden under the long grass having been there all winter. The rake was extremely rusty. We removed it, cleaned up the wound as best we could and I gave her a Ledum 200. Her mother wasn't quite sure about not going to the hospital, but when her daughter was obviously relieved by the medicine I had given and had stopped screaming, she relented and continued with the remedy twice a day for five days. The remedy relieved the pain and shock very quickly and the wound was completely healed in three days. This was a child who has never been vaccinated at all and she is still alive and in excellent health eight years later.

The routine way in which highly toxic tetanus shots are given to people in hospital for every kind of injury is absurd. Very often the effect of the tetanus shot is far worse than the wound itself. The arm swells up, becomes stiff and very painful for up to ten days after and there may be innumerable side-effects.

Another friend's daughter accidentally stepped on a wine glass that had been left on the floor of her living room. The cut was nasty and her parents took her to casualty. She was immediately given a tetanus shot, even though the wound was clean and had not come into contact with any soil or dirt of any kind (just a little white wine!). Her arm swelled up hugely and was stiff and extremely painful for two weeks. The wound on her ankle healed up nicely and was far less painful or worrying than the tetanus shot. She had also been previously vaccinated with the DPT.

I would like to see much better guidelines as to the use of the tetanus vaccination and, certainly, the right to choose without being lectured or made to feel irresponsible if opting for non-vaccination. If a parent, or anyone for that matter, refuses this shot then they usually have good reasons and their decision should be respected.

Sarah – born 1986
Sarah was brought to me in 1993 with eczema, mainly on her legs, but also some in the folds of her arms. On looking more closely into her case I found that she also slept badly, had a very poor appetite, had hard pea-sized glands at the back of her neck, always breathed through her mouth, and had a permanently blocked nose. She was also very thin, had dark rings around her eyes, a grey complexion and unstable energy. Other than this, Sarah was a happy, sensitive and much loved child.

Her family history revealed allergies in the mother's family and asthma in the father's and, most interestingly, her mother's mother had had diphtheria badly as a child and nearly died. Since recovering from the diphtheria, however, she has led a healthy, full life with no other serious illnesses to this day!

Sarah's personal history was very interesting. She had a good birth and was breast-fed up to nine months. She was born with dry skin and a hip problem, but was otherwise healthy.

The eczema appeared after her first set of vaccinations at the age of two months and was severe. She had all her other vaccinations, including one for measles, to which she had a violent reaction. The day after the vaccinations she became extremely listless, began moaning, vomiting, developed a high temperature and became very pale. This state lasted five days after which she recovered.

Sarah's mother felt worried and angry that she had not been given any warning at all that this might happen, and decided not to have her second child vaccinated against this disease.

From then on Sarah began to suffer from repeated tonsillitis, croup, severe ear infections, mainly in the left ear, and mild asthma and, of course, was prescribed lots of antibiotics. At three years old she contracted chicken pox and soon after that the eczema began to disappear. The immune system was given a chance to react naturally to the chicken pox which had also cleared out some of the ill-effects of the previous vaccinations.

She was fine then for a while until her pre-school boosters, after which her eczema returned. Her tonsillitis and ear infections had persisted and she underwent a tonsillectomy and adenoidectomy at six years old under general anaesthetic (a very common scenario for many seven-year-olds in the UK!)

The first thing to do was to clear out the initial vaccinations as these had caused the problems. I gave her a homoeopathic dose of the DPT 10M, a much higher dose than normal since she had been given the vaccination a long time ago. This was followed a week later by a single dose of homoeopathic Polio, in the 200th potency, then a constitutional remedy in a low potency so as not to aggravate the eczema.

I saw her five weeks later and her eczema had initially got a lot worse and then speedily better. It was then only dry skin with some white discolouration, a considerable improvement. She was sleeping soundly and was well in herself, although she still had a poor appetite, her glands were still swollen and she was still constantly mouth-breathing.

I gave her a single dose of Morbilinum 30, a remedy made from measles and told her mother to continue with the constitutional remedy. There was a lot of work to be done to get Sarah better. She needed homoeopathic Tetanus, remedies for the anaesthetic and the operation and, of course, sound constitutional treatment. It took about a year to restore her to health. The greater the lapse in time between the vaccinations and the start of homoeopathic treatment, the more difficult it becomes to repair the damage done.

I saw Sarah again two months later and her skin had cleared completely except for a little on the backs of her hands: a good general improvement. I gave her some Baryta Carb.1M to continue improving her health and some Hydrastis 30 to help her put on some weight.

I saw her again a month later and her skin was absolutely clear. Her energy had improved, she looked better, but was still lacking in appetite and was slightly constipated. I then gave her Alumina 30 to finish clearing out the ill-effects of the vaccinations, and some Silica in a high potency.

She was then very well for the next year and I did not see her again until December 1994. In that November, against her mother's wishes, she had been given the MR vaccination at school.

A couple of weeks after having the MR Sarah was ill again after having been clear for over a year. She got a bad, croupy cough, was full of mucus and had been given antibiotics. She had lost her appetite again and was clingy and miserable. However, the skin had not been affected this time and was still clear, showing that it was the first set of vaccinations, the DPT, that had triggered the eczema. I gave her a homoeopathic remedy made from the MR, something to clear out the antibiotics, and another high dose of Silica to finish it all off. She has been fine ever since.

Lawrence – born July 1993
Lawrence was brought to me in August 1993, at one month old, simply with mild milk spots on his face. He was basically a lovely baby and was brought to me as I had treated nearly all the members of his African family with good

results. I gave him some homoeopathic Silica and he was fine.

However, in October of that year he was brought back again and was covered in nasty eczema from head to foot. He was also constipated, was not sleeping well and was sleeping on his stomach with his bottom in the air. He had a dry cough and was very snuffly.

He had had his first vaccinations at two months old. He had reacted violently to them and his mother and grandmother were sure the vaccinations had caused his ill-health. They had tried to discuss this with the doctor but he said it was impossible and refused to look further into the matter.

Mothers nearly always know what is happening to their children but are rarely listened to. It was quite obvious to me that the whooping cough part of the vaccination had done most of the damage, especially as there was a very strong family history of asthma and eczema, which always contra-indicates the use of this particular vaccination.

I gave Lawrence the clearing-out regime and advised his mother not to give him any more vaccinations. The family was relieved to be heard. I saw Lawrence again three weeks later and his skin was 50 per cent better but he was still sleeping badly and had a loose cough. I then gave him some homoeopathic Tuberculinum and saw him again four weeks later. His skin was now 75 per cent better, he had grown a lot and put on weight, but was still not sleeping and his father said he thought he was hyperactive. I then gave him a constitutional remedy, Calcium Sulphate, and a month later the eczema was completely gone. He was sleeping better, but was still not perfectly well.

This is such a common story, but it is rare for me to see a baby before it has its vaccinations. So many children who have this family tendency to asthma and eczema are born with a susceptibility in the lungs and skin and the vaccinations trigger their weak points. Most children go on to have two more sets of the DPT, Polio and Hib and then the MMR on top. Lawrence was very lucky to have avoided further bombardment and recovered fairly quickly without cortisone. Most children like this have eczema for years with all its consequent suffering for child and parents.

Jordan – born August 1991
Jordan was brought to me in December 1993 with persistent chest infections. Every cold went to his chest, and he would cough up thick mucus which would

catch in his throat and cause him to vomit. He had a good birth but had to have his lungs sucked out and was kept in hospital for ten days. He was given antibiotics just in case he might have developed a chest infection. You can clearly see an early susceptibility or weakness in his lungs from birth. He was then fine until his first cold at eight weeks old. He had all his vaccinations with no apparent reaction. At eight months he had a bad ear infection and had to have three lots of antibiotics to clear it. From that point on he had antibiotics every three months for one infection or another. He then had the MMR at thirteen months. He had a permanent dry cough and runny nose that became infected regularly and was treated with antibiotics. He was extremely thirsty, very hot and sweaty and had pea-sized glands, at the back of his neck, which never went down. He slept and ate well but was slightly hyperactive and ran everywhere. He was very loved and well cared for and generally a pleasant and sociable child.

I gave him the standard homoeopathic clear-out for the side-effects of the vaccinations and some Natrum Sulph, 30 to clear some of the chronic catarrh. I saw him again a month later and he had made a complete recovery in all respects. After taking the Natrum Sulph, he had streamed with green catarrh and become constipated and aggressive. He was then given MMR 200, DPT 200, Polio 200 and Hib 30. He had two colds soon after which only lasted three days, and he has been completely well ever since and needed no more treatment.

Lucy – born August 1991

Lucy was brought to me in December 1991. She is a wholly unvaccinated child and is an interesting case as she gives a clear picture of susceptibility.

She was born nine weeks premature after an emergency caesarean. She weighed 2lbs 4oz and had to be incubated for nine weeks. During this time she had some enteritis, with some bleeding from the anus, and an X-ray showed a shadow on her lungs. She recovered and was eventually sent home with a bronchodilator (theophillin) to help her breathe as her lungs were immature and very weak. Her mother had sometimes forgotten to give it to her and said she felt it made no difference anyway. Her mother brought her to me to help build her up. She was eating and putting on weight and I gave her some Silica 6 drops to be taken daily for a month. I saw her again five months later and she had been very well up until two weeks previously, when she had developed a cough and cold that had got considerably worse in the last couple of days.

She was brought into my office in her mother's arms. She was limp, extremely feverish, and sweating profusely. She had a temperature of 102°F and a thick, teasing cough with clear sputum. She was having fits of coughing and was vomiting mucus afterwards. The child was obviously distressed, her lungs were full, and she had a rapid heartbeat. She had all the symptoms of full-blown whooping cough.

I gave her Aconite 30 to be taken two to three times a day and asked her mother to ring me in a couple of days. Lucy responded well to the Aconite and was making a good recovery.

I saw her two weeks later and she was considerably better, now just a little chesty. She had put on weight and looked bright and happy. She had been to the hospital where her progress was being monitored, as she had been a premature baby, and the doctors could not understand how she had suddenly become so well. They even insisted she have a chest X-ray and a visit with a top specialist to see if they could work out what was going on. She had the X-ray, a lung capacity test and a sputum test and everything was fine.

I gave her some homoeopathic X-ray 30 to clear the side-effects of this and some more Aconite (but a stronger 200 potency) to take if she became ill again.

I saw her a month later and she was doing fine, although her lungs were still a bit rattly. In herself she was happy and well. She had been to the hospital again, where the doctors pronounced her well, but insisted on giving her another X-ray that showed nothing. I gave her another X-ray 30 and some Silica 200 to strengthen her generally.

Lucy was well until the family went to Spain for a holiday, where the weather was cold and rainy. She got chilled and caught a cold, which immediately went onto her chest. Again Aconite was prescribed with good results, followed by a Silica 10M to strengthen her generally.

She was completely well until October 1992 when she got another cold which also affected her chest badly. Aconite 200 again worked beautifully. From that point on, with every change of season the same thing happened and, again, Aconite cleared the problem.

In between Lucy was extremely well and happy, had developed well, and was in every respect a normal child. During her first two years I also gave her *Tuberculinum* twice to strengthen her lungs and also various other remedies, including a remedy made from each of the childhood diseases to strengthen any susceptibility there.

Her mother very early on decided not to vaccinate Lucy at all and now she is a lovely, healthy four-year-old. Her mother is very pleased to have made that decision.

There was TB in the family in a grandparent, plus diabetes and pancreatic cancer. The TB in the grandparent had set up a weakness or susceptibility in the child, inherited through the genes. If she had been given the whooping cough vaccination, perhaps she would not have had whooping cough but she would most certainly have become a chronic asthmatic. Her early experiences in the hospital and subsequent visits to the doctor showed that they were keen to use asthma drugs from a very young age and, with her premature birth, this was really the direction she was going in. Having whooping cough allowed her immune system to develop and become strong, although she definitely needed help to get through it.

She has gone from strength to strength ever since and the last time I saw her, in February 1995, she was extremely well and was brought in for a verruca.

I spoke to Lucy's mother, again this year, 1999, who said she was really pleased that she decided not to vaccinate. Lucy is now 8 years old and stopped having her seasonal bronchitis completely from 3 years old. She also has another child, 4 years old, unvaccinated, who is never ill. Lucy has been in excellent health and her mother said she has become "incredibly robust".

CHAPTER FIVE

POLIO, HIB, C-STRAIN MENINGITIS, AND THE BCG

Polio, Hib (Haemophilus influenza type b) vaccines and C-Strain Meningitis are given at the same time as the DPT: at eight, twelve and sixteen weeks. Polio is given again with Tetanus and Diphtheria as a pre-school booster at four to five years and again at school-leaving age, sixteen to eighteen years. The BCG (tuberculosis vaccine) is sometimes given to new-born babies if there is a local epidemic of tuberculosis but usually it is given at puberty, between eleven and fourteen years.

Polio
This vaccination is given orally, on a sugar lump, and contains three types of live, attenuated (diluted) poliomyelitis viruses cultured in tissue taken from monkeys' kidneys. It is the only vaccine that is given orally and in this way, is the only one that mimics the normal route the disease would take if contracted naturally. There has been a lot of controversy over this vaccination, focusing mainly on a dispute about the relative efficacy of the live vaccine developed by Sabin (taken orally), and the killed vaccine developed by Salk (injected under the skin).

The live vaccine, which remains active in the bowel for several weeks, was designed first to try to remove the severe side-effects of the killed vaccine (convulsions and brain damage) and, second, to ensure the continuation of the disease and promote mass immunity.

As the virus is still live for several weeks it can be passed through the faeces of anyone infected and be given to susceptible people. Most at risk here are the elderly, or people with weak muscles or nervous systems. There have been many cases of elderly or susceptible members of a family contracting polio from the stools of a recently vaccinated baby, as well as cases of paralysis and death.

There have been many successful court cases following this type of infection, in fact there have been so many court cases in the USA that the American authorities there are seriously considering re-introducing the Salk method, using the killed virus injected under the skin – however, this method has so many adverse side-effects, it is doubtful that it will ever be adopted again.

The disease itself is only dangerous to infants over three years old. Up to that age the disease is synthesised extremely well by the infant and the symptoms are only those similar to a mild digestive upset, so often go unnoticed. If an infant develops polio before the age of three, there is very little risk of it developing into paralysis and the child is then naturally immune for life. It is only after this age that there are possibilities of a serious disease developing with paralysis, muscle wasting and even death. Again, if homoeopathy is used, any weakness of the muscular or nervous system should be strengthened early on, but as with any disease, susceptibility is the key. In the 1950s there were terrible outbreaks of polio in the UK. Many people remember it being a terror of their childhood and everyone knew someone in their street who had had the disease. Again, it was the post-war period, nutrition was still poor, and people were in a state of recovery, both materially and spiritually. Interestingly it was also a time of mass vaccination of this disease and it is questionable whether this was a natural outbreak from poverty and mal-nourishment or whether in fact the epidemic was caused directly by the vaccination.

Why can't this disease be allowed to die like so many of the other formerly fatal diseases, such as scarlet fever and smallpox?

The polio viruses are spread mainly by hand-to-mouth contact of infected faeces, or through the digestive tract by ingesting contaminated food or water. They can also be spread by coughing and sneezing, but this is rare.

Symptoms appear from four to fourteen days from initial infection and are very similar to those of flu: aching muscles, fever, sore throat, headache, gastrointestinal disturbances and general malaise. At this stage the symptoms are covered very well by a remedy called Gelsemium, which is a common flu remedy.

A Homoeopathic remedy given in the early stages, when these symptoms appear, could pre-empt the disease from becoming more serious. This is where it is so useful to have a first aid kit of Homoeopathic remedies at home and many diseases can be prevented in this way.

As always, if first aid given at home does not appear to be resolving the situation then professional help must be sought.

The virus is commonly dealt with, in the early stages, by the healthy immune system and excreted through the bowel. The faeces remain infectious for several weeks after, even through the individual has recovered.

On the whole this is the extent of the disease; in susceptible people complications can occur. Remember, where there is susceptibility to the disease, there is also susceptibility to the vaccination.

Complications

1. Meningeal irritations causing vomiting, stiff neck and a positive Kernig's sign (spasm of the muscles at the back of the knee while extending the leg from the knee in a recumbent position).

2. If the virus enters the brain stem it may cause difficulty swallowing or coughing, nasal speech, difficulty in speaking and interference in the eye muscles, causing a squint, as well as flaccid muscles in the face.

3. Paralysis due to the virus entering and affecting the nervous system, which can come on at any time between two to seven days from the initial infection, can be mild or severe. The disease is at its worst twenty-four hours after the beginning of the paralytic stage and if this is dealt with successfully a full recovery is made. Symptoms of paralysis are flaccid muscles, loss of tendon reflexes and retention of urine. There is the possibility of death from lack of oxygen if the respiratory muscles become involved.

4. Wasting of limbs due to prolonged paralysis of muscles. Recovery from this is gradual and the patient may need physiotherapy. Some permanent deformities of limbs may occur due to nerve damage by the virus, which in turn prevents the natural growth of that limb.

Haemophilus Influenza Type B (Hib) and C-Strain Meningitis

There are several types of meningitis, viral and bacterial. Hib is a bacterial strain which is most harmful in infants from three months to four years old. C-Strain meningitis is also bacterial and affects, more commonly, older children. This is the meningitis that has been causing many teenage deaths around the UK in recent years.

The meningitis bacteria is weak and does not live outside the body for more than a few minutes. It lives harmlessly in the mucus at the back of the nose and throat in one in ten people. Most people are not affected by the bacteria at all. They are simply carriers with no symptoms and the bacteria will die over time.

In one person in a thousand, if the immune system is weak the bacteria can pass into the blood stream causing the serious disease known as meningitis septicaemia (C-strain) or into the brain causing Hib. Scientists are presently trying to ascertain what makes certain people susceptible and not others but, as discussed in the chapter on the immune system, susceptibility is individual and a healthy, mature immune system will deal with most infections in their initial stages.

As the bacteria does not live for long outside the body it is only spread by close contact. With Hib it is spread by infants who have very close contact with each other so that nasal mucus gets passed from one to the other. Also by wiping the nose of one and then another child with the same handkerchief. With C-Strain, although the above still applies, it is more likely to be passed by kissing or by prolonged close living conditions.

Good, simple hygiene does a lot to prevent the spread of this disease.

The Hib vaccine was introduced into this country in 1990. It is cultured in cattle tissue and is given as a separate injection into the thigh muscle at the same time as the Polio and D.P.T. – at eight, twelve and sixteen weeks. The vaccine has already undergone several changes as the early types were incompetent and had many side-effects.

C-Strain Meningitis vaccine is a very new vaccination, it is genetically modified and will be available from the Autumn of 1999. It will be given at the same time as D.P.T., Polio and Hib and offered to older children, especially University and College students, where the disease seems to be doing the most harm. This will bring the total number of shots given to children under two years of age to 21.

Symptoms
The symptoms of both these diseases are similar. They can come on very suddenly which is why prompt action of whatever nature is important. The first symptoms are high fever with vomiting, severe headache and stiff neck, shivering, cold hands and feet, rapid breathing, intolerance to light, drowsiness, stomach and joint pains and, in the case of C-Strain, a rash.

In babies there may also be a bulging fontanelle (the soft spot on top of the head), a stiff body with jerky movements, a fretful shrill cry when disturbed, loss of appetite and pale blotchy skin.

There are two Homoeopathic remedies which, if given early on, can prevent the disease from becoming more serious. These are Belladonna and Aconite.

Belladonna is specific for meningitis and covers the high fever without sweat, throbbing headache, blotchy skin, drowsiness, stiff neck, glassy eyes and loss of appetite.

Aconite symptoms are similar, high fever, shivering, headache, but the patient is more restless and anxious than Belladonna.

Both remedies cover both types of meningitis and, in fact, the symptoms are very similar.

Complications
1. With C-Strain meningitis if the bacteria enters the blood stream, it rapidly causes septicaemia. The toxins in the bacteria damage the blood vessels and blood leaks out under the skin causing a red, blotchy rash. A good test for this is to press the skin with a glass tumbler. If the skin remains red despite the pressure, then this is a sure sign of septicaemia and action must be taken.

2. Damage to the blood vessels in turn reduces the flow of blood to the important organs such as the liver and kidneys which may cause them to fail and the patient to die.

3. Hib. is very similar but the more serious complications are in the brain rather than the blood. Here you would be more likely to see the stiff neck, with an inability to move the head backwards or forwards, high fever and screaming as the bacteria affects the meninges of the brain. Young children have unstable nervous systems and are easily affected by inflammation of the brain causing epileptiform convulsions similar to epileptic fits.

4. Inflammation of the meninges can lead to hydrocephalus, which is an abnormal collection of fluid in the skull. The upper part of the head increases in size out of proportion to the size of the face and body and the

bones of the skull separate slightly. Normal brain function is interfered with causing dizziness, listlessness and irritability, which may lead to mental subnormality.

5. There may also be permanent nerve damage causing deafness, blindness or squint caused by the initial inflammation of the meninges. Death may occur from paralysis.

The BCG

This vaccination is intended to prevent the disease tuberculosis. It is made from live attenuate bovine tubercle bacterium cultured in tissue taken from cattle. The name "BCG" stands for "bacillus Calmette-Guérin", after the two Frenchmen who developed the vaccine.

Like many of these infectious diseases, tuberculosis (or TB) is very much a disease of poverty and war. In Europe, TB was at its worst at the turn of the twentieth century and much intelligent and dedicated work has since been undertaken by scientists and doctors to gain an understanding of this disease and of its cure and prevention. There has been, and still is, a huge amount of positive research being done world-wide.

In the UK the disease went into rapid decline after 1940, due largely to the end of the terrible wars that had ravaged Europe previously, as well as to the improving standard of hygiene, nutrition and general health-care at that time.

The BCG vaccine, which was first introduced in France in 1908, seems to have had little effect in preventing the disease. The whole vaccination programme is now considered to be confusing the issue rather than helping, as anyone who has had a Heaf or Mantoux test becomes sensitised to TB and future tests are therefore inconclusive. This makes it difficult to chart the spread of the disease. A simple X-ray of the lungs shows up any previous infection and eliminates the need to present toxic material into the bloodstream.

It takes about one hundred years to develop a natural immunity within a community. In Europe this time has elapsed. This vaccination is one of the least important, especially as its effectiveness is very suspect. However, since 1987 TB has been on the increase, mainly in the US where poverty (especially homelessness), drug abuse and alcoholism are rapidly increasing. It is also one of the commonest causes of death in people with AIDS, whose weak immune system simply cannot deal with the bacteria at all, and this is contributing to the higher incidence of the disease in recent years. This is a political issue. Governments need to recognise the implications of homelessness and poverty and to instigate creative measures to alleviate the problems, as was done in the 1950s and 1960s. This is more important than increasing the vaccination programme; whose vast cost could be diverted into positive measures to alleviate poverty and homelessness, which in turn would reduce the incidence of TB.

It is now up to local authorities in the UK to decide whether or not to pursue the vaccination programme in schools and a lot of authorities are opting out. Where the vaccination is being given, it is done between ten and fourteen years old and the Heaf test is conducted first to see whether the child already has antibodies to TB.

The Heaf test is performed by means of a "gun" consisting of 6 small needles in a circle. It is used to puncture the skin of the forearm and contains a small amount of purified tubercular tissue. If a lesion appears at the site of the test within six weeks, then the individual is deemed to already have antibodies to the disease and will not need the vaccination itself. Such individuals should also be offered an X-ray to confirm the test, as a previous infection of TB will show up as a shadow on the lung.

The Mantoux test is similar except that it is done by injection deeper into the tissue, and is designed for people who are suspected of having the disease.

Common side-effects of the vaccination are adenitis (inflammation of the adenoids) or keloid scars (hardened, lumpy tissue) at the point of vaccination. More subtle symptoms include increased sweating, bad temper, period pains, allergies, lack of concentration, a desire to run away and low grade lung and skin affections, all of which often disappear after a dose of a homoeopathic remedy made from TB. Interestingly enough, these are common characteristics of most teenagers – could there be a relationship here?

The disease itself is caused by an air-borne bacterium known as *Mycobacterium tuberculosis*. It used to be known as consumption or phthisis and is now commonly known as TB. The earliest recorded cases of TB were noted by Hippocrates in 460 BC. It is highly infectious and caught by inhaling infected droplets coughed out by someone who already has the disease, or by inhaling infected dust, or ingesting infected milk. The bacterium can lie dormant in a dried form in dust for many weeks, and become reactivated when inhaled. It is impossible to destroy it by freezing or drying, and it does not decay with age. The only way to render it harmless is by sunlight.

Most cases of TB are symptomless, as a competent immune system will deal with it very effectively. The immune system first initiates all the normal functions (phagocytosis, etc), and then ingeniously encapsulates the bacteria with scar tissue containing a high proportion of calcium. This effectively cuts off the disease from the rest of the body and stops its spread. These capsules are known as "tubercles" and can be clearly seen by X-ray. This procedure allows the individual to lead a completely normal life, even though the evidence that he or she has had tuberculosis is there. In later years it is possible for the tubercles to break down and re-activate the disease, commonly in a situation of poverty or where the immune system is compromised by drug abuse, alcoholism, or immune deficiencies such as AIDS.

This is why a healthy, well-informed immune system is so important. The only case of TB I have seen in practice was in a 17-year-old boy who had been vaccinated at the usual time – 14 years old. His infection was serious and he lost half a lung. He had become susceptible through taking drugs, drinking and disco-ing too much and the vaccination made no difference whatsoever.

A Swiss doctor, Dr Jean Elminger, recently published a very interesting book called "Real Medicine" on the perils of vaccinations and in it he describes having worked as a young Doctor in a TB sanatorium in Switzerland. He observed that those who died of this disease tended to be the ones who *had* had the vaccination, whereas the unvaccinated ones usually survived.

If the bacteria are inhaled or ingested by someone with an incompetent immune system, then the following symptoms appear:

Symptoms
Initial symptoms are slow in onset and consist of mild fever, loss of appetite (anorexia), general malaise, fatigue, a tender red rash mainly affecting the legs, known as *erythema nodosum,* enlarged lymph nodes, a dry cough, noisy breathing (stridor) and difficulty in breathing (dyspnoea).

Complications
1. Enlargement of lymph nodes may block an airway causing that part of the lung to collapse.

2. Abscess of the lungs due to necrosis of lung tissue from the disease.

3. Pleurisy (inflammation of the lining of the lungs), or pleural effusion (accumulation of fluid in the lining of the lungs).

4. Broncho-pneumonia. This is characterised by a rapid heart beat, high temperature, difficulty in breathing, lack of oxygen and a wet cough containing purulent sputum. The patient may die from toxaemia or heart failure.

5. Bronchiectasis. This is an abnormal dilatation of the bronchioles causing a wet cough with a profuse amount of foul-smelling sputum, high fever, weight loss, finger clubbing (deformity) and anaemia.

6. Emphysema. This is an over-distension of the small alveoli in the lungs causing a lack of elasticity of the lungs, which in turn causes a lack of oxygen to the blood supply, especially on exertion. Death may ensue from this complication by lack of oxygen to the heart causing heart failure.

Modern drugs control TB very effectively. But they in turn have their own side-effects and the patient will become increasingly weak. It is preferable to have a well developed, competent immune system in the first place!

Ivo – born May 1994
Ivo was brought to me in January 1995 suffering from a continuous cold, a wheezy chest and vomiting at least once a day. He had a poor appetite and constipation, only going to the toilet every third day. He was mainly having cow's milk, his sinus area was puffy and congested and he could not breathe through his nose. The glands in his neck were permanently swollen and his hearing was slightly low. Apart from that he was a pleasant, well looked-after baby, happy and sociable and growing well.

He suffered projectile vomiting from birth and developed thrush at seven weeks, showing that his immune system was already weak before the vaccinations. There was no apparent reaction to the vaccinations but at four months old he developed bronchiolitis and an ear infection at the same time, for which he was given antibiotics. Two months later he was in hospital with bronchiolitis again and was treated with Calpol and a nebuliser (asthma treatment). A month later he had tonsillitis and was again taken to hospital (no treatment was given this time). The tonsillitis recurred two weeks later, after that he was brought to me.

This again is a very typical picture. Even though Ivo was only eight months old he had already developed lots of minor illnesses which had turned into chronic conditions; no really serious diseases, but a string of low-grade problems that could easily lead to glue ear, tonsillectomy or adenoidectomy, possibly asthma and bowel problems later on, all of which would be exacerbated by vaccinations to come.

I gave him DPT 200, Polio 200 and Hib 30, followed by his constitutional remedy Calcium Carbonate 200. I also advised his mother to cut down on formula milk as it was obviously overloading his liver.

A month later Ivo came back and was considerably better. He had had one bad cold but dealt with it well and his nose was clear. He had a mild reaction to the Hib, was irritable and restless, but only for twenty-four hours.

The vomiting had stopped, his chest was clear and his appetite had improved. He looked much better and was less puffy. By clearing the side-effects of the vaccinations Ivo was brought into his real self, a happy, well-loved and healthy little boy.

Here you can see that the immune system was not functioning properly in that it was failing to clear infection. The child then developed permanent, low-grade problems. When the immune system was released or unblocked by the remedies it cleared the body of toxins by means of a streaming cold, but this time the cold came to an end.

Michael – born November 1992
Michael was brought for homoeopathy in July 1993 suffering from eczema in the creases of his knees and arms which began at three months old. Apart from this he was in good health, slept and ate well, and was happy and settled.

There was eczema in the family: his mother suffered with eczema and asthma, his mother's grandfather also had eczema and in his father's family there were lots of skin allergies.

He was given the initial vaccination clear-out, had a strong reaction and was seen again in August 1993.

After the homoeopathic Polio 200 he had diarrhoea for five days, was whiney and upset, developed nappy rash and the eczema got worse! Two weeks later the eczema had gone, and when I saw him in August he was left with just very mild dry skin. In every other way he was completely well. He was given a dose of Sulphur 30 and seen again in September 1993. The skin had cleared completely and he was full of energy, sleeping well, and was playful and happy. This is another case of a child who needed nothing more than to have the side-effects of the vaccination cleaned out.

Jasper – born August 1989

Jasper was brought to me in May 1993 suffering mainly from tiredness and irritability. He did not have any particular illness, but for a three-year-old had very poor energy and would lie on the couch and watch TV between 12.30 and 3.30 every afternoon. He was fine in the morning until lunch time, when he would become irritable and destructive, after which his energy would drop dramatically (ME symptoms?) He was also congested nasally and snored at night, was not thirsty at all, tended to overheat badly in warm weather, was emotionally oversensitive and had regular tantrums. He ate well, but was very fussy and had to have the food separated on the plate before he would eat it.

He was born with jaundice but recovered and was fine soon after. He had no apparent reactions to the vaccinations. At six months he had an ear infection that was treated with antibiotics and, at ten months, he began to get repeated chest infections for which he was given several courses of antibiotics and underwent lots of tests. All these problems eased off and his last winter was quite good. He had no more infections, but low energy and general discomfort instead.

There was a lot of asthma in his family: his mother was asthmatic, his father's mother also had asthma and his mother's grandmother had died from an asthma attack. His father's brother had also had severe eczema as a child.

I gave him the homoeopathic clear-out and saw him a month later. All the symptoms had cleared after having a couple of colds that he dealt with quite easily. His energy was normal for a three-year-old and not so variable, his nose had cleared and he was much happier – his energy had been released by unblocking his system and he had come back to himself.

I heard from Jasper's mother in August 1995 that he had remained completely well and needed no more treatment.

CHAPTER SIX

CONCLUSION

I hope that you have found the information contained in this book helpful and informative. It is a matter of choice whether or not you vaccinate your child and whatever choice you make is completely acceptable.

What I am trying to present here is a way of dealing with children's health and the prevention of disease through homoeopathy. As I have said before, to use homoeopathy takes a lot more thought and responsibility but, for those people who want this type of health care, it can work very well and creates a positive state of health in the child.

If you decide that you do not want to take that kind of responsibility and go ahead and have your child vaccinated, don't worry. Few children suffer serious side-effects and most survive intact. It is not only the vaccination that does the damage, but also the susceptibility of the individual. If you are unsure whether or not to vaccinate (which in my experience is most parents' situation) then have the vaccinations, or some of them, but also use a homoeopathic remedy before and after to help clear the side-effects.

There are no hard and fast rules and it takes a lot of courage and conviction to bring up a wholly unvaccinated child. Although it is very difficult to prove that the vaccinations do damage some susceptible people, I have witnessed enormous benefits to my patients in the clearing of side-effects of vaccinations through homoeopathic treatment.

It was through observing the difference between vaccinated and unvaccinated children that I was prompted to investigate this issue and to try to work out what actually happens when a child is vaccinated. The children on my books who have not been vaccinated I hardly ever see, as they are so healthy. These children are generally bigger, have far less infections of any nature, are clear-eyed, clear-skinned, bright, well balanced and intelligent. They have everything one would expect from living in a clean, sophisticated environment. Vaccinated children are rarely as fortunate.

The most convincing evidence I can present in support of non-vaccination is to describe some of the children who have never been vaccinated and whose parents have made the choice to use homoeopathy as their main system of medicine. To this end, and as a parting gift to any of you who are considering not vaccinating, I shall now introduce you to ten children of varying ages whose parents have chosen not to vaccinate, and a follow-on five years from the first edition of this book. The "introductions" are in the form of completed questionnaires that I sent to a large group of parents. They are presented as written and speak for themselves.

JACK

1. What made you first think about not vaccinating your child?
   We discovered that Jack was allergic to dairy products and I had read that children showing allergic reactions are most likely to have bad reactions to vaccinations.

2. How did you find the information you needed to make a decision?
   I read a variety of pamphlets to be found in clinics (my GP's and also alternative clinics, e.g. acupuncturists). Also, talking to other people, including yourself and other parents.

3. Please explain briefly any anxieties or worries you may have had making this decision.
   We were worried about Jack being at risk from dangerous diseases such as polio and tetanus. We were also worried about it being a problem to other parents, playgroups and eventually schools.

4. Did you have any problems with the medical profession over this decision?
   Yes, my GP was very unhappy with this decision and every time I visited the surgery he would talk to me about our decision and try to persuade me otherwise. However, he never presented a new argument, and the points he raised we already felt we had thought about carefully. Interestingly, the

67

health visitor who saw Jack more regularly, changed her attitude as time went on, as she saw how healthy Jack was and she said that this was generally true of other children who hadn't been vaccinated.

5. What benefits do you now think your child had by not vaccinating?
We believe the main benefit Jack has had is that his system has had a chance to build up his own resistance to diseases which has resulted in a healthy body which is rarely unwell.

We also feel that he is more alert and energetic than other children of the same age who have been vaccinated, but this is a difficult thing to measure.

6. Has your child been well and have you noticed any differences between your child's health compared to children you know of the same age?
Jack is now two and a half and in all that time he has had three tummy bugs (two whilst being abroad), about five common colds and two bouts of conjunctivitis (following the colds) and that's all. I would say that generally he is healthier than other children the same age.

7. If your child is old enough to answer questions, what does he/she think about not having been vaccinated? (It would be very interesting to hear their opinions.)

1. 5 years on – do you feel you made the right decision not to vaccinate?
Yes, in fact, we feel even more confident about our decision now than we did at the beginning.

2. Is your child in good health?
Yes, Jack is in excellent health. He rarely has colds. Even when he had glue-ear he never got an ear infection (without using antibiotics).

3. Have you observed any differences in your child to other children in their peer group who were vaccinated?

4. Any other comments?
Attitudes towards vaccination from our doctors seem more relaxed now than when we first decided not to vaccinate Jack. Perhaps this is because we so rarely need to see him!

THEO

1. What made you first think about not vaccinating your child?
   I myself had not been vaccinated and had not suffered any terrible illness. My Mum made the decision after my eldest sister who had had all the vaccinations was prone to catching anything going around. Also an American cousin of mine was severely brain damaged at eighteen months old as a reaction to a measles injection. My Uncle and Auntie had to give permission for the life support machine to be switched off. Mum also said she had no faith in preventive medicine.

   I shared this belief. My son Theo seemed so pure when he was born, it didn't seem right to inject diseases into such a young body, giving his immune system no chance to function for itself.

2. How did you find the information you needed to make a decision?
   My sister, an aromatherapist, sent me some articles she had read on vaccination. I read articles at my pregnancy yoga class and two books on the vaccination dilemma.
   I couldn't believe what I read as nowhere along the line had a doctor or health visitor warned me of any risks or impressed upon me that there was any choice.

3. Please explain briefly any anxieties or worries you may have had making this decision.

I was anxious about the enormity of the decision so soon after Theo was born. Becoming a mother for the first time was a big enough event without all the incredible pressures of having him vaccinated so early. Almost all the other parents around me were having their babies vaccinated; not liking it, but unaware of any other choice or the alternatives. I felt as though I and my husband were the only parents around questioning the decision (I've since met like-minded parents). No health visitor sat me down to tell me about any risks, or gave the full information, I was simply sent an invitation to go along to the clinic for the vaccinations.

4. Did you have any problems with the medical profession over this decision?

This question made me laugh – I had such problems with the medical profession. As I had read so much on the subject, I didn't take my homeopath's advice to lay low with my decision.

When going into the clinic, I stated we didn't want Theo to be vaccinated and backed it up with information and statistics. I was accused of starting the plague all over again; asked how I would feel if Theo died of whooping cough etc.; then referred to the chief health visitor. I received the same treatment, told I was a risk to other families and was referred to her superior.

As I really believed we'd made the right decision, I went along. By the end I wished I'd taken the advice and laid low. None of the above could back up their information with facts but used the heavy-handed approach I listed above. I didn't feel my decision was respected.
[Since then I am continually lectured by GPs about my decision.]

5. What benefits do you now think your child had by not vaccinating?

I think Theo has a much, much better, stronger immune system. He's happy, healthy and extremely bright. I really think we've given Theo a gift, especially in this day and age.

6. Has your child been well and have you noticed any differences between your child's health compared to children you know of the same age?

Theo is well, healthy, happy. He had chicken pox when he was two years old and hardly had any spots, didn't itch at all and was happy throughout. The only inconvenience was the quarantine. Two of Theo's friends who had been vaccinated had chicken pox at the same time. They were covered in spots, itched constantly and both suffered high fevers for a few days. Also once the chicken pox cleared, they both had a strange unexplained (by the GPs) rash which spread over their bodies, starting at their heads and moving down, lasting an hour then it was gone. Theo didn't have this at all. Since starting Nursery, there is always something going around with children repeatedly off sick. Theo rarely catches anything and if he does, only mildly.

Theo has always been very alert, speaking sixty or more words by eighteen months old.

7. If your child is old enough to answer questions, what does he/she think about not having been vaccinated? (It would be very interesting to hear their opinions.)

1. 5 years on – do you feel you made the right decision not to vaccinate?
I have never regretted my decision. Theo is 7 now and extremely healthy and active.

2. Is your child in good health?
Yes. In the last 3 years at Primary School he has missed 2 days through illness, where I have kept him off with the mildest of symptoms to prevent it developing into anything worse. Each time I have felt slightly 'conned' as Theo has bounced through the day.

3. Have you observed any differences in your child to other children in their peer group who were vaccinated?
Certainly at school and with his cousins, who have been vaccinated, Theo doesn't seem to catch the 'bugs' going around. At Christmas Theo shared a room with 4 of his cousins. Each day, one by one, the cousins fell foul of an awful flu/gastric virus; with fevers, conjunctivitis, diarrhoea etc and I watched and waited for Theo's turn. He had a 'funny tummy' as he put it for a day, still eating, running around, no fever etc. He has an incredible immune system!

<u>DAVID</u>

1. What made you first think about not vaccinating your child?
    A combination of factors.

    1. A strong feeling that vaccination had contributed to the physical and emotional problems of my elder son.

    2. As a homeopath in training at the time, I knew that there were better ways of dealing with any childhood illnesses David was actually likely to get.

2. How did you find the information you needed to make a decision?
    It would have been harder (see 1:2 above) for me to have found information in favour of vaccination!

3. Please explain briefly any anxieties or worries you may have had making this decision.
    None – he is such a healthy child that I feel if he does get anything he will be well equipped by his own level of vitality and with the help of homoeopathy, and throw it off and be better for it.

4. Did you have any problems with the medical profession over this decision?
They had already given up on me over my preference for a home birth. As – now – a professional homeopath they do give my views some respect.

5. What benefits do you now think your child had by not vaccinating?
It's difficult to separate the benefits of being a "homeopathic baby" – the product of four years of homeopathic treatment for both parents – from those of being unvaccinated. He is a triumph for both! His level of energy is excellent and he has stamina, both physically and mentally, as well as a sunny disposition. If he gets ill he throws it off dramatically and quickly – he doesn't suffer from chronic anything – no snuffles, glue ear, recurrent ear infection or wheeziness, which are in his family background.

6. Has your child been well and have you noticed any differences between your child's health compared to children you know of the same age?
See no. 5 – his nursery teachers, carers and family (even blasé grandmother with three older grandsons) regard him as something quite exceptional.

7. If your child is old enough to answer questions, what does he/she think about not having been vaccinated? (It would be very interesting to hear their opinions.)
David isn't, but my eight year old considers it most unfair that he had to be vaccinated (before I knew about homoeopathy), and is quite sure he never will be again!

1. 5 years on – do you feel you made the right decision not to vaccinate?
Yes. David has stayed really healthy and when he has occasionally had a fever or childhood illness he has thrown them off quickly.

2. Is your child in good health?
Yes, nothing chronic at all.

3. Have you observed any differences in your child to other children in their peer group who were vaccinated?
Things don't "hang on" with David – he has a cold (sometimes) and recovers. No runny noses, lingering coughs etc.

4. Any other comments?

   He has excellent concentration, is doing well at school and is very friendly and adaptable. The evidence is that this is not entirely genetic!

KARIMA

1. What made you first think about not vaccinating your child?
   I was aware that vaccinations had side-effects. As an asthma sufferer myself, I realised my daughter had a risk of inheriting my weak lungs, and I knew that vaccinated children had more colds and chest infections. Otherwise, I just wanted to make the best decision with regard to her health and give her the best possible start in life. This meant boosting her natural immunity – not undermining it.

2. How did you find the information you needed to make a decision?
   While I was pregnant, a friend gave me a book that has revolutionised my life – Homoeopathy for Mother and Baby *by Miranda Castro. I would recommend this to all mothers-to-be. It offers a lot of clear, useful advice on mothering in general (from pre-conception onwards) as well as the more specific homeopathic treatments. It helped me to understand the principles of homoeopathy and the fact that our bodies have a powerful defence system which, once understood, can be enhanced and work very efficiently in maintaining peak health. It also expressed reservations regarding vaccinations, but advised the reader to consult a professional homeopath – I subsequently started to see a homeopath (since the seventh month of pregnancy) to ensure my baby would have the best possible health right from the womb. I found out more about vaccinations in discussions with my homeopath, as well as from literature revealing facts*

*about immunisation that are well guarded by the medical establishment –
one which gave me greater insight and understanding about the reasons
why vaccinations are not only dangerous, but also ineffective, was* The
WDDTY (What Doctors Don't Tell You) Vaccination Handbook – A Guide
to the Dangers of Immunisation *– (available from 4 Wallace Road, London
N1 2PG).*

3. Please explain briefly any anxieties or worries you may have had making
   this decision.
   *The decision not to have my daughter vaccinated was fairly easy – I was
   lucky to be seeing a homeopath who offered an alternative homeopathic
   immunity enhancer (I therefore consider that I have had Karima
   immunised, though not vaccinated). Had I not had the support of my
   homeopath, I might have felt a lot more frightened and helpless in making
   this decision. It is a brave step to take in the current medical power
   structure, as many of my friends who I consider to be enlightened about
   conventional vs. holistic therapies still opted for "just one" vaccine (either
   polio or MMR, or whooping cough, depending on which one someone had
   succeeded in scaring them most about). But I had read the WDDTY
   handbook and seen programmes about the sequels of so-called safe
   vaccines – I opted for ZERO-JABS!*

4. Did you have any problems with the medical profession over this decision?
   *They did do their job and try to scare me. But my mind was already made
   up. I switched GPs to one closer to home after Karima was born and was
   lucky that they (the women practitioners) were quite supportive, or at least
   not undermining. What I find most intimidating are all the posters staring
   down at you from the walls in the waiting room – it's like a very well
   engineered campaign to force mothers to feel they have no option, and that
   they are neglecting their child's health by not having them vaccinated –
   that you risk killing your child. It is extremely intimidating, even terrifying
   – they tell you that it is your responsibility morally, but what they don't tell
   you is that you have a choice not to do it – that they are actually lying to
   you when they make out that the vaccines have no side-effects and often
   don't even work. They even had a series of advertisements on Jazz FM (I
   had to stop listening to that station in the end), where they told you that
   you were irresponsible if you didn't immunise your baby. It is real
   propaganda – what I realise is that if you don't have your child vaccinated,
   you have to read a lot about it just to fight back and defend your decision.
   It makes me really angry because it's peoples' lives they're messing up, and*

it's not a matter of free choice in the end as the medical establishment is putting so much money into promoting vaccinations.

5. What benefits do you now think your child had by not vaccinating?
Karima is now sixteen months old. She hasn't had a single vaccination. She is generally happy, independent and very sociable. It is hard to say what benefit she has had from not being vaccinated at this stage, except the obvious one that neither of us had to go through the trauma of her being jabbed. I also made sure I breast fed her for a long time (until fifteen and a half months) to enhance her natural immunity, and she certainly enjoyed that experience. She has had problems with teething, which leads to mucus in her nose and chest, and coughing, but she has always responded well to homeopathic treatment, and I feel quite confident that she is, on the whole, a very healthy little person.

6. Has your child been well and have you noticed any differences between your child's health compared to children you know of the same age?
See previous answer.
Most of the children I know of her age are not vaccinated, or barely ("just the one") – and lead healthy lives, eat well (no sugar, etc.). It is hard to notice, except that a lot of people comment on what a healthy-looking child she is.

7. If your child is old enough to answer questions, what does he/she think about not having been vaccinated? (It would be very interesting to hear their opinions.)
If she could say anything, Karima would, I'm sure, feel proud that her mum had the sense and the guts to stand up to the social pressure and not tamper with her health. Had I had any choice in the matter I would have liked to be given the same chance, and maybe (very possibly) I would have stopped suffering from asthma and bronchitis a long time ago.

8. Any other comments?
Probably to be included under Q.2. Fact (in WDDTY): "It is not that the vaccines don't work, but that they work imperfectly"… "They might confer a temporary immunity and wear off at the point when exposure to the disease is most dangerous, or have risks, including permanent disability and death, far higher than those of contracting the disease naturally." Whatever the case, it is clear we are not just dealing with a simple little decision, but a very big one, both for individuals and governments, and

one that has many serious implications.

Also, people must realise they have a choice in this matter – I have heard so many stories of intimidation, it just makes me realise how desperate the authorities are to convince us that vaccination is the only option (if they have to pressure us so much it suggests a great risk to me). One woman I know was told she had to vaccinate her child, or she wouldn't be allowed to send her to school.

It is true that vaccination is compulsory (by law) in France. I don't know what the situation is in other countries – it's worth checking out if you want to emigrate. I know I will not move to France while my daughter is at school if she has to be vaccinated. To me this is a breach of individual freedom – imposed by the UN and the WHO with their "extended immunisation programme" to ensure that every person in the world is vaccinated by the year X. As I see it, they have got their priorities wrong and should invest the money into improving standards of hygiene, making drinking water available to all, etc.

1. Five years on, do you feel you made the right decision not to vaccinate?
   Yes. Karima is now 6 and, although there have been times when I have worried about how I would cope if she contracts an infectious disease, I have never felt that she would be better off if she had been vaccinated. On the contrary, I feel very strongly that I have done the right thing by her in terms of minimum risk, as vaccinations can have serious side-effects, as well as the less obvious chronic depletion of the immune system, and who knows what long-term disastrous effects. I am, however, slightly worried about exposing her to situations in which she may benefit from protection, such as travelling, as she may be going on a trip to Turkey, for which the NHS recommends immunisation against Tetanus, Polio, Hepatitis A, and Typhoid. Although I should be able to boost her quite adequately, and with no side-effects, through homoeopathy, I will probably be worried about her contracting anything at all until she is back in my care (as I will not be travelling with her). There is always an underlying lack of faith in the gentler ways, as I am aware of having been brought up in the allopathic system, which has impressed on me – against my better judgement – the sense that allopathy is sound and reliable, like the men in white coats! In fact, the only times I have been made to feel any doubt about my decision

not to vaccinate have been exposure to men in white coats, who have attempted to make me feel that I am an incompetent single mother who doesn't know what she is doing and who is taking serious risks with her child's health/life. I have therefore found it essential to develop a network of supportive people, such as homoeopaths, cranial osteopaths, etc., to discuss my doubts and confirm that I am being totally responsible in this decision and my healing methods.

2. Is your child in good health?

    Yes and no. She has constitutional problems which take longer to resolve, but her body is good at sorting things out and she is strong, lively and happy.

    I only became aware that Karima had serious hearing problems when we left home and moved from London to Bristol. I had been aware that she was not responding when spoken to, and was concerned that she had behavioural problems, as well as speech difficulties. I thought it was just her stubborn personality, as she likes to do everything in her own particular way – from eating habits, to inability to do puzzles that her friends (minimally vaccinated) could do in no time, to clinginess and a strong determination, combined with despair and despondency, shyness, and an eccentric and airy Aquarian personality (she is quite often in a world of her own). She passed the 2-year assessment at the doctor's, who stated her hearing was fine. She attended a child psychology clinic for behavioural assessment, as the nursery also drew my attention to communication difficulties. There appeared to be no serious problem, until we moved to Bristol and her hearing clearly deteriorated. After having a lot of wax syringed out (first softened with Mullien oil), we were lucky to acquire a new health visitor who advised I should take her to the Children's Hospital for a hearing assessment, as she was still not hearing well. Karima was diagnosed with severe glue ear, a condition which appears to be very common amongst children in Bristol, due to the greater degree of dampness in this city. They recommended she have a hearing aid or grommets by September, when she was due to start school in Reception, unless there was a noticeable improvement. She has since been receiving cranial osteopathy in addition to constitutional homoeopathic treatment, particularly through acute phases, and her diet is as dairy-free and healthy as possible. As a result of this treatment, she was given the "all clear" at her second assessment, and has been improving steadily since then, although she has got worse over the winter season. She is expected to improve as she grows and her Eustachian tubes get larger and start to tilt down more, enabling the catarrh to flow more freely from her middle ear. The diagnosis came as a shock and a relief, which is often the case with glue ear. Children need to be diagnosed as early as possible so that they may receive beneficial treatment, and all the evidence indicates that Karima may have had compressed hearing channels from birth, and it appears she heard most of the time as though both her ears were blocked up. It was unfortunate that she passed her 2-year health check, as this meant the problem went undetected and was addressed incorrectly in terms of her difficult behaviour.

When she was younger, Karima had a tendency to develop asthma when she got a chest infection, which would develop quite easily from a cold. Through homoeopathy she has now developed the capacity to clear chest infections without them turning into asthma. When she was about two, a local GP had tried to convince me that she should be given a Ventolin (Salbutamol) inhaler, which I felt they were handing out much too easily and I strongly objected to, as I thought this would only cause her to be stuck in the condition rather than overcoming it. She developed eczema for the last quarter of 1998, which coincided with the asthma clearing out of her system. I treated the eczema in ways that would relieve it without suppressing it, with soothing oils and Crab Apple (Bach Flower Remedy). Now, both the asthma and eczema have cleared, which is very exciting in terms of her progress.

She developed acute conjunctivitis in December 1996, when we left home, which was the only time in her life she ever took any allopathic remedy, as I was unable to take her to a homoeopath at the time. She recently developed conjunctivitis again, following her last homoeopathic remedy, which caused the symptoms that had been suppressed by the antibiotics two years ago to clear out as she gets stronger. (Both times according to the same pattern, starting in her left eye, then onto the right eye).

Otherwise she contracted a gastro-enteritis virus last December, although she wasn't too bothered about it. However, she went on to contract the next passing virus, and developed a persistent dry cough, which didn't really bother her either.

On the whole, Karima is full of vitality, even when she is ill, and she does fight things off well. It is very rare for her to miss school, which she loves, and she is pretty resilient to onslaughts on her health. She has a delightful personality and is very confident in her own wisdom. Basically I think that, although Karima has had, and still has, problems with her health, she has greatly benefited from not being vaccinated, in fact I dread to think how bad she might be if she had been vaccinated. She has great inner strength that might have been stifled, and her proneness to catarrh would probably have been exaggerated. She has had problems which she has succeeded in clearing, and others which are being cleared, and when she does contract a passing bug, she carries on with a sparkle and clears it out. I think she is in the process of laying the foundations for very sound health throughout her life. Furthermore, she is growing up in a holistic context, learning about the different remedies and essential oils, Rescue Remedy and Rescue Cream, Hypercal ointment, etc. She knows that natural things are best, and chemicals are to be treated with caution.

2. Have you observed and differences in your child to other children in their peer group who were vaccinated?

   One thing I have noticed is that it is not always obvious whether a child has been vaccinated or not. There are cases where I am convinced that there must be a connection between a child's chronic poor health (physical, emotional, or mental) and the fact they were vaccinated, for example the chronic "naughty" ones or bullies at school, those who have had their noses cauterised to stop the recurring nose-bleeds, or those who suffer from multiple allergies. Many vaccinated children enjoy apparently good health and show levels of vitality which occasionally makes me wonder about the vaccination issue. But I have noticed a tendency for more subtle lack of resistance, maybe they get more colds or coughs. However, Karima has not enjoyed perfect health, so I can hardly proclaim the obvious benefits of abstaining from the vaccination programme, although as I stated above, it is clear to me that she has benefited and continues to do so.

   When she was three, a TB virus was detected in her nursery, and everybody concerned had to take a Heaf test to determine whether or not they had been affected. Karima sailed through, and cleared two tests at six-week intervals, while many children were compelled to endure months of strong medication. I cannot say for sure, but somehow I felt this was a result of her strong immune system, which wasn't confused by having to deal with the onslaught of vaccinations, and was thereby free to face this particular one and shrug it off. I believe that most, if not all, of the affected children had received the routine vaccinations. Another child who had only received minimal vaccinations also escaped unharmed. Karima even thought nothing of the Heaf test, which has been her nearest experience to being jabbed to date, and she still role-plays about being "clicked" – yet many of the children who had endured vaccinations were traumatised by the thought of being jabbed again.

On the whole, many vaccinated children can enjoy apparently equal good health if they lead a healthy life-style, eat a balanced diet with little toxins, are not surrounded by pollution and stress, and are treated with minimum allopathy. My concern is about the basic suppression of the immune system right from the start, about the potential damage that can result immediately from the vaccinations and, if these effects are avoided, the less obvious immune deficiencies that deplete the body's innate ability to fight off infection.

3. Any comments?
   If people choose to vaccinate, this decision is understandable, as it is still very difficult to choose in the current climate. However, I am convinced that many conditions could be avoided by abstaining from vaccinations. It appears safer on the surface, but the veneer is full of cracks. More people are now becoming aware of holistic medicine and leading healthier lives, so hopefully there will be a greater acceptance of the inadequacies of vaccinations, and the gentle, side-effect-free alternatives.

   And finally, a little-known fact: GPs get paid more if they fulfil a certain quota of vaccinations (the same goes for the cervical smear tests), which certainly reflects the pressure imposed on the medical profession to sell the vaccination programme to the best of their ability, rather than seek to find the best solution for their patients!

<u>MAY</u>

1. What made you first think about not vaccinating your child?
When May was born she was a perfect little human being. I had been on a strict cleansing diet before becoming pregnant so I knew I was passing on few toxins to her. I read an article on the statistics surrounding vaccination and the occurrence of the diseases they should protect us from. There was no real evidence to prove that the decline of these diseases was due to vaccination. Why fill my child with eight diseases she will probably never catch? At eight weeks old!?! NO WAY.

2. How did you find the information you needed to make a decision?
A close friend gave me some literature but I didn't need to read it. There was also an article in a Sunday colour supplement which explained very well what effect a large number of vaccines have on a developing immune system. I didn't need any further information anyway – by instinct I knew I was following the best path for my child.

3. Please explain briefly any anxieties or worries you may have had making this decision.
The only "What if?" I had was around polio. There had been two recent cases of adults catching polio from the nappies of children in the process of vaccination. I was wary of May having contact with such children. In

fact she contracted measles from a child who had recently been vaccinated. But I was not about to let fear rule the health of my child. I know polio can have severe side-effects but I knew the likelihood of her contracting it in the UK were slim.

4. Did you have any problems with the medical profession over this decision?
   I had heavy lectures from three of the GPs at the practice we attended. They tried to use fear to make me change my mind. When I explained to them I had a degree in biochemistry and was confident in my decision they left me alone. Even without their support I was clear about my actions.

5. What benefits do you now think your child had by not vaccinating?
   She is hardly ever ill. She's had measles which she recovered from in about 4 days and chicken pox which she got over in just over a week. She wasn't poorly with either illness. She gets an occasional cough/cold but again, they clear up very quickly. On her second birthday she was 3 ft ½ inch tall. She's just turned three and she is 3 ft 6 in! She wears clothes for a six year old, counts to twenty and can recite her alphabet without much work on my part. She is precise in her speech and can hold quite advanced conversations with most people she meets. She is physically strong – happily lifts a 2kg dumbbell – and can walk long distances (< 1 mile) without complaint. I cannot say for sure whether this is due to non-vaccination, but compared to children of her own age who are vaccinated, she is well in advance. I have yet to meet her match physically and mentally. I have met one child but she is six months older than May. The main difference is her speed of recovery when compared to other children.

6. Has your child been well and have you noticed any differences between your child's health compared to children you know of the same age?
   See above.

7. If your child is old enough to answer questions, what does he/she think about not having been vaccinated? (It would be very interesting to hear their opinions.)
   Unfortunately, May can't quite grasp this concept yet!

8. Any other comments?
   I'm just really pleased that I believed in myself because EVERYBODY was against my decision – even May's father, so I had to "pull rank". As I said, I will never know for sure but I'm happy not to take the risk and experiment

with my child's life. I am still working on building my own immune system, she won't have to go through all the ailments I do.

1. 5 years on – do you feel you made the right decision not to vaccinate?
   I definitely made the right decision in not vaccinating Araba. MY 7 yr old daughter is nearly 4'9" and wears size 4 shoes!!

2. Is your child in good health?
   Araba May is in excellent health. This winter she's had a cough and snotty nose but she has not been poorly with it. she's strong and fit. Walks, swims, rides ponies. She is confident and positive.

3. Have you observed any difference in your child to other children in their peer group who were vaccinated?
   She seems well ahead of her peers. She tends to get on with older children. She is awake and aware of the vast universe around us. School, unfortunately, does not seem to stimulate her enough

4. Any other comments?
   She often does projects at home using library books and me! We meditate together and she's great company. She keeps me going when things seem tough! I cannot prove that her advanced personality is only due to non-vaccination but I believe her energy goes into her development rather than fighting all those vaccinations.

BEN

1. What made you first think about not vaccinating your child?
We have both long been in favour of the gentle and holistic approach of homoeopathy. We also read reports of the possible negative effects of some vaccinations for some kids, and that there was as yet no established way of foreseeing these reactions. The complete lack of long-term research material on the overall safety of conventional vaccines was just one of the factors that made us seriously question the wisdom of it.

2. How did you find the information you needed to make a decision?
Questions 1 & 2 are obviously linked as we didn't fully make up our minds to seek an "alternative" vaccination programme until we heard about you through a friend. We found most of the literature on the subject in Watkins bookshop, and you guided us to a couple of books. We've also stumbled across some articles in the dailies (Guardian? Independent, I think), which were generally very toned down for obvious reasons.

3. Please explain briefly any anxieties or worries you may have had making this decision.
Yolande had much more than I did, but that's mainly a reflection of the different ways we reach a decision. In the end we both did this with considerable trepidation for the following reasons:

a) On the surface it looks as if the mainstreamers have most of the cards as far as "concrete" evidence goes. But when you begin to peel away the false claims (such as vac programmes being responsible for the decline of a particular epidemic, etc.), and the misleading implication that these programmes are "safe" (by whose/which criteria?) our decision became an article of faith based on what we thought was common sense. Now I've yet to meet anyone who has been able to hold this kind of dalliance with the Unknown without also stirring up a storm of self-doubt and fears that the "rest" may be right after all.

b) Peer pressure: some friends thought – and probably still think – we were mad to take such a risk with our child.

4. Did you have any problems with the medical profession over this decision?
    Ties in with 3 because if there is one organisation that is going to stir up anyone's anxieties on a delicate issue such as this it's the Medical Profession. We were fortunate in that we have a relatively understanding GP, but the rest, such as the local Health Authority, Queen Charlotte's Hospital, the health visitors, even the GP's receptionist, were completely uncomprehending about our decision. So much so that it was impossible to have the most basic discussion on the subject. It was a totally foreign language to them. One nasty little incident at Ben's hearing test involved Yolande being heavily pressurised to write a note to the local Health Authority giving the reasons for not vaccinating. I'm glad for their sakes I wasn't there!

5. What benefits do you now think your child had by not vaccinating?
    It's impossible to quantify the benefits of "vaccinating" the homeopathic way. Given the absence of definitive material in this area (and given that it may always be this way), we really acted on gut conviction as much as common sense. It cannot be right to stuff the body with viruses using the method that a conventional vaccination does and not expect some long-term side-effects on the body's immune system. We believe, feel, hope that we have honoured Ben's system by using a method that stimulates it the natural way. But neither of us feels self-righteous about what we've done!

6. Has your child been well and have you noticed any differences between your child's health compared to children you know of the same age?
    Ben seems to be far less ill and to have fewer problems (despite his reluctance to sleep) than any other child we know who has been

vaccinated. This is obviously a purely subjective observation. But we would like to think that his state of health is partly attributable to his homeopathic treatments (not just the "vaccination" powders). There are other factors to consider, such as his diet (Yolande's very careful and thoughtful), prolonged breast feeding, or even as the sceptics would have it, sheer good fortune. But whichever way you look at it, Ben's health is astonishing, and on the two or three occasions he's been ill, he's shaken off the lurgy-burgy in next to no time. Also because he has not been jabbed up the armpits, he has no fear of the doctor and her waiting room, no experience of intrusion, and no association that a trip to the doctor's surgery means pain (all further benefits). This is somewhat incomprehensible to those who administer it, which in turn baffles us. Do they not remember?

7. If your child is old enough to answer questions, what does he/she think about not having been vaccinated? (It would be very interesting to hear their opinions.)

8. Any other comments?
   Yes, two points that you will probably be covering anyway.

   a) *Anyone making a decision in this area should be prepared to walk into what feels like a collective wall of rage. People who haven't the faintest idea of the issues involved, and even less interest in finding out about them, haven't hesitated in accusing us of a variety of heinous crimes, from the fairly mild objection that we are indulging our irrational fears, to the off-the-handle assertion that we are putting the vaccination plan and the whole country at risk. The one that really goes for the jugular is that we are putting our child's health at risk on account of a selfish ideal. This is primitive, emotional stuff and hardly provides the basis for making a calm, considered judgement. And there is no doubt that the power of the mantra combined with the sheer number of people saying it makes one feel awfully isolated. What would be useful is some kind of helpline/association where the arguments for and against can be presented dispassionately. Perhaps there is one already? If so, it doesn't make itself known very effectively.*

   b) *Another thing we didn't reckon on is the social dimension of going homeopathic – especially school. We only discovered by coming here that if you go and live in another country, France being a good example, you may find your child is not allowed to go to school without vaccination papers. This means you may have to lie, cheat or simply face the prospect of your child being treated as a pariah. Nor can you be safe if you do manage to slip through the net. In one case, we learned of a child being herded in with the rest of its age group for a vaccination top up without the parents being informed!*

So it's important to stress that the commitment to go homeopathic must be total, because it's not a once-only decision. As long as the intolerance – no let's be honest, prejudice – carries on at its present level, you've got to live with your decision until your child is at least an adolescent. Frankly, having learned how leaky the pro-vaccination lobby's arguments are – as well as how breathtakingly amoral the pharmaceutical industry is – we stand by our choice.

1. 5 years on – do you feel you made the right decision not to vaccinate?
   Absolutely, every time they go to their GP they feel "what a waste of time".

2. Is your child in good health?
   Ben is in excellent health although suffers from minor skin problem. When he was 3½ years we were living in France and he and his unvaccinated younger sister both got whooping cough and were fairly ill with it. However, they recovered much better and quicker than the children who gave it to them who had all been vaccinated. Before this Ben had suffered with a weak chest and had had several bouts of chest infections. Since having the whooping cough his chest is much stronger and he no longer gets chest infections.

3. Have you observed any differences in your child to other children in their peer group who were vaccinated?
   It is hard to comment on this objectively as I adore my children and think they are the best. Also it's not always easy for Ben to always be different from his peer group as he is already bigger than they are and has led an unusual life despite only being 6 yrs old.

4. Any other comments?
   We feel more and more that we have chosen the best paths for our children

by using Homoeopathy. However we could not have done it without the expertise and support of our Homoeopathic practitioner. To be able to ask questions and get advice along the way is emotionally invaluable when the rest of the world thinks differently. We also feel the orthodox medical profession does not have the understanding and resources of diagnosis of holistic medicine and often do not know what to do except give their standard stock medicines that compartmentalise the symptoms. We have no problem now with our decisions and now have two completely unvaccinated children who are growing into healthy, intelligent beings.

LOUISE

1. What made you first think about not vaccinating your child?

   I do not remember the first time I became aware about the possibility of not vaccinating children. It must have been before becoming pregnant. I knew unvaccinated children and their parents even then, and I was impressed by how blooming they were. The decision my partner and I eventually made started as mainly a gut reaction in tune with our way of thinking about health. I have a profound distrust for long-term medical treatment, from past family experience and orthodox medicines, which I only take when too scared not to. Both Andrew and I are lucky to be quite healthy and value the positiveness of it.

   I felt good during pregnancy, and took homeopathic remedies to preserve my and my baby's wellbeing in those months. Louise had a natural childbirth, without drugs, and was never under undue stress during her home birth. It seemed that she had the most perfect wholesome little body, and I was very unhappy about polluting it.

2. How did you find the information you needed to make a decision?

   The actual decision was more difficult to make, and I searched for the relevant information supporting both cases. I got all the local health authority leaflets, and read mainstream baby and child care type of books.

I also got a pep talk by the health visitor in favour of jabs.

Also a book entitled Maximum Immunity, and a whole issue of the New Scientist, which detailed the workings of the immune system. The last two convinced me of the paramount importance of maintaining a healthy immune system, in an environment where pollution and stress are getting worse. They also highlighted that most of the up-and-coming illnesses were related to quirky failures of our immune system to function properly, e.g. cancers, or auto-immune illnesses.

Then I read various publications, from "What Doctors Don't Tell You". All of them stressed the risks and frequency of side-effects of vaccines, one by one, and the low rates of success of each in achieving lasting immunisation in their little patients. They also gave away the manipulation of official figures, and the real scenario relating to the disappearance of immunisable illnesses such as diphtheria, small-pox.

I read about a "Parent Register" which puts parents in touch with each other when their children have contracted a childhood illness, so that other children can catch the illness and obtain life-long immunity to it naturally. I joined both WDDTY and the register.

Finally, we went to my homeopath, who explained how she has successfully treated measles in unvaccinated as well as vaccinated children, and how polio is not dangerous in children under two, and then only translates as a kind of gastric fever. She talked about the health hazards which Louise would be most likely to face in the 21st century, such as pollution. We decided after then, that Louise would have a better future without jabs

3. Please explain briefly any anxieties or worries you may have had making this decision.

    My partner and I went through a lot of heart-search on the subject of vaccinations or no vaccinations. Either way, we were rather awed at the responsibility we were taking. Vaccinating seemed like straightforward poisoning/polluting of a clean new body, but the anti-vaccination option was regarded by many people around us as a completely foolish decision, which left Louise a sitting duck for any fatal infectious disease, waiting to attack her at any moment.

For months, I listened anxiously every time Louise coughed, in fear of the whoop of whooping cough. Measles, meningitis, polio and tetanus were equally worrying. I checked her temperature every time she vomited, and scrutinised her body for purple marks, in fear of meningitis. I refrained from taking her to the public baths for fear of contracting polio from a vaccinated baby, and worried about her muscle movement for days when the doctor suggested a tetanus jab after she cut herself on a baby food tin. Each time, I read the relevant entries in the medical books, sometimes in the middle of the night, and rang my homeopath first thing the next day for reassurance.

I am quite sure that I will continue this checking for months to come, although things are a little less frightening now that she is not a tiny baby any more.

4. Did you have any problems with the medical profession over this decision?
I did not get into trouble with the medical profession, probably because I do not see them very often. When I went for Louise's three months check up, I made up an excuse that I was going on holidays for a while and could not face the jabs then, and at the nine months check up, I came out with my decision to my health visitor. She was quite accepting, and I think that she has come across it before.

5. What benefits do you now think your child had by not vaccinating?
By not being vaccinated, Louise hopefully avoided the emotional and physical distress of the vaccinations on the day, the risks of short- and long-term reactions to the vaccines and their components, (hyperactivity, autism, fits) and the long-term health hazards present when an immune system is compromised before it gets a chance to develop, (tumours, cancers, auto-immune illnesses).

I hope that she gained physical strength to face up to illnesses, pollution, etc.

6. Has your child been well and have you noticed any differences between your child's health compared to children you know of the same age?

Louise meets up regularly with a group of toddlers of similar age. I have noticed, over the last fourteen months that I have known these children, that they have all (except one – also unvaccinated) had at least two or three chest or ear or intestinal infections. Most of these were prescribed antibiotics, and many of the little girls went on to develop thrush. Some children seemed to be ill for stretches of months, suffering from one thing after the other.

Over the same period of time, Louise never had an infection, never was prescribed antibiotics, never had thrush. She did have a few colds: one went onto her chest, was treated homeopathically, and lasted a couple of weeks at the most. It is only with the last, current one, that she had her first fever one night, about 39 degrees. I am also treating this homeopathically, and she is on the mend. All her other colds were head colds, and only lasted a few days.

It could be that my natural mistrust of doctors means that I do not rush to their surgery as often as other mums, and her colds remain undiagnosed and unprescribed conditions. However, I think that I am as anxious as the next mum about my baby's health, and I would look for professional advice if confronted with the symptoms Louise's little friends had. I'd rather think that her good health is a reality.

7. If your child is old enough to answer questions, what does he/she think about not having been vaccinated? (It would be very interesting to hear their opinions.)

8. Any other comments?
   My main reservation on the subject of non-vaccination, is that the decision is often made in the context of homeopathic (or other alternative) care, which is less readily available and much more expensive than the NHS standard medical care.

   I am not sure what my choice would be, if my child was suffering from one of the immunisable illnesses, when the only place I can take her in an emergency is a hospital. I expect that the pressure to follow orthodox treatment would be at its greatest, when the only professionals at hand for support at a time of disarray, and who could examine Louise, would be medics. They might even pressurise me into vaccinating, or at least guilt trip me!

   I also worry about being able to always afford frequent visits to the homeopath, should Louise develop one of the infectious illnesses.

1. 5 years on – do you feel you made the right decision not to vaccinate?
I am still not absolutely sure, although I believe it has been good for Louise so far. However, should circumstances change, Andrew and I might get her selected vaccinations now that she is older and stronger.

2. Is your child in good health?
Yes, but Louise seems to have inherited slight hay fever from her father. She sneezes violently for about 5 minutes and her nose produces lots of discharge upon waking in the summer months.

3. Have you observed any differences in your child to other children in their peer group who were vaccinated?
Louise enjoys good health and has no other allergies (asthma, eczema etc) – she has an average of 2 colds a year, which have never given rise to infections of the respiratory system. To date she has never required antibiotics. She is more "Tonic" than many of her friends, very sure of herself physically and very energetic. I think she is a well adjusted kid who enjoys life. Some of her friends are not so lucky and are either less energetic or more often afflicted by colds etc.

CHRISTIANNA

1. What made you first think about not vaccinating your child?
   Whilst I had my first child, Joseph, vaccinated with great reluctance (altho' not MMR or Hib) I noticed a definite decline in his health afterwards. Therefore, this gave me the drive to definitely not have Christianna vaccinated.

   I am also very lucky not to have been vaccinated as a child nor my other six brothers and three sisters and we're all very much alive and well and have strong constitutions!

2. How did you find the information you needed to make a decision?
   Apart from advice from my mother and my own motherly instincts on the matter, I managed, after much searching, to find books and articles on the subject.

   I also spoke to other like-minded parents and found Tina who could support me and my children's health without the use of harsh drugs.

3. Please explain briefly any anxieties or worries you may have had making this decision.
   I had very little worries, as I had read information on the subject, together with personal past experience of the side-effects of vaccination on my son

and other parents' children.

4. Did you have any problems with the medical profession over this decision?
None whatsoever really apart from a raised eyebrow! Whilst my doctor did not support my arguments, she accepted it was my decision!

I got the impression when speaking to the medical profession that they did not really know the facts that I was stating and there was no way anyone was going to get a two-sided view on vaccinations from them (no doubt a financial loss in doing so!)

5. What benefits do you now think your child had by not vaccinating?
Christianna is the picture of health. She has a sparkle in her eye and a skip in her step! She rarely gets anything, but when she does she fights it off really well and symptoms do not linger. I have noticed that by allowing her body to get any childhood illnesses, she has become stronger and fitter afterwards, as though the illness was an actual stepping stone in her development.

In comparison, Joseph suffered ill-health after vaccination, i.e., recurrent swollen glands, runny nose, heavy catarrhal head, chest infections and low energy. However, thankfully, with the help of alternative medicine, he has good health now in general.

6. Has your child been well and have you noticed any differences between your child's health compared to children you know of the same age?
The only major concern I have had is when Christianna contracted whooping cough. However, it was not severe and the homeopathic help given worked well. There was only one week of coughing bouts and during that time I never felt that Christianna was in any danger. I noticed how strong and resilient she has become since she recovered from it.

Generally, though, she is very much different to children of her age. She seems brighter, happier, healthier and without the constant runny nose, sallow skin/red cheeks, coughing of so many children around.

7. If your child is old enough to answer questions, what does he/she think about not having been vaccinated? (It would be very interesting to hear their opinions.)

8. Any other comments?

I feel very angry that the Government does not give a two-sided view on the topic of immunisation/vaccination. Parents should be allowed the real facts and therefore total freedom to make an informed decision whether to immunise, e.g. the current info on measles is totally one-sided.

As a sixth child in a family of ten children all not immunised at childhood, not one of us has had asthma, eczema or any of the other lingering chronic diseases around today.

1. 5 years on – do you feel you made the right decision not to vaccinate?
   Most definitely.

2. Is your child in good health?
   Excellent

3. Have you observed any differences in your child to other children in their peer group who were vaccinated?
   Much healthier, stronger and vibrant.

4. Any other comments?
   No comments as I am absolutely sure I have done the right thing and now also have another unvaccinated child also in perfect health.

LAWRENCE & TARA

1. What made you first think about not vaccinating your child?
   Whilst pregnant I visited a naturopath who was against vaccinations. His reasoning made complete sense to me although I was still affected by the traditional way of thinking.

2. How did you find the information you needed to make a decision?
   Books provided by friends. By listening to friends and professionals – both from the medical world and alternative practitioners.

3. Please explain briefly any anxieties or worries you may have had making this decision.
   I thought long and hard on the decision re. vaccinations. I listened to both sides of the argument from friends and professionals. This made it a difficult decision at the time. With the benefit of hindsight I have no doubt I came to the right conclusion regarding my children's health.

4. Did you have any problems with the medical profession over this decision?
   I was seen as extremely irresponsible by the South African medical professionals I came into contact with. They tried their utmost to change my mind, using mainly scare tactics. Since moving to England, to my surprise, no-one has challenged my decision.

5. What benefits do you now think your child had by not vaccinating?
I think my children have benefited by having healthier immune systems. Adding vaccine seems to confuse the body's natural response to disease. My son had measles aged three. He was quite ill, although I noticed a consequent strengthening in his overall ability to fight illness. This was particularly noticeable where his allergy to wheat and dairy products was concerned.

6. Has your child been well and have you noticed any differences between your child's health compared to children you know of the same age?
Both my children are in excellent general health. They suffer from the occasional bout of flu or cold, but I do not take this as a bad sign! My children are now ten and eighteen.

1. 5 years on – do you feel you made the right decision not to vaccinate?
Yes, I feel it was not an easy option because when Lawrence had measles it was very scary at times and was very bad. However, he has been tons better ever since.

2. Is your child in good health?
He is in superb health and he is growing into an intelligent and very focussed 15 year old.

3. Have you observed any differences in your child to other children in their peer group who were vaccinated?
Seems to have far more energy than his peer group – who are often very tired.

4. Any other comments?
Just pleased I didn't vaccinate.

JOE

1. What made you first think about not vaccinating your child?
   I have looked after children for the last thirteen years, and have seen so many of them suffer due to having been vaccinated, and decided not to have Joe done – plus I'm a great believer in children getting most illnesses and fighting them naturally.

2. How did you find the information you needed to make a decision?
   Read several books on the subject, for and against. Came to the conclusion that not vaccinating was better, and the information for vaccinating your child wasn't too convincing for me. Too many questions not answered.

3. Please explain briefly any anxieties or worries you may have had making this decision.
   I did not have any worries about my decision, I just knew that I was doing the right thing for my son. Gut instinct told me I was doing the right thing.

4. Did you have any problems with the medical profession over this decision?
   My GP was extremely unhelpful and told me in no uncertain words that I was extremely irresponsible and if my son got any of the illnesses it was my fault.

5. What benefits do you now think your child had by not vaccinating?
Joe is so much better at fighting off infections, he's extremely healthy and always aware when he might be catching something and straight away asks for his lavender or olbas oil and eats plenty of fruit. When he does get a cold it sometimes hits him really hard, it goes to his chest or he may get a bad cough, but he never wheezes or has ever had a runny nose.

6. Has your child been well and have you noticed any differences between your child's health compared to children you know of the same age?
Most of the children in Joe's class at school have asthma, those who had the measles booster suffered from a severe cold, high fevers and three children ended up with a bad case of measles. Out of thirty children in one classroom, only ten children turned up after the booster for that week. Joe very rarely gets ill.

7. If your child is old enough to answer questions, what does he/she think about not having been vaccinated? (It would be very interesting to hear their opinions.)
I saw what the children in my class went through when they had the measles booster. A lot of them cried and were scared. I'm glad I did not have to go through that. Some of them got very sick. I don't like needles, and my doctor isn't very friendly. My friends think I'm very lucky.

1. 5 years on – do you feel you made the right decision not to vaccinate?
Yes, just seeing how healthy Joe is and that he never gets ill, except the odd cold which soon goes.

2. Is your child in good health?
Excellent health and very happy.

3. Have you observed any differences in your child to other children in their peer group who were vaccinated?
Even now in Joe's new school children are always off with some virus or another which Joe never catches. A lot are Asthmatic.

4. Any other comments?
Had a bit of pressure from my doctor down here, but soon put him straight, now they leave me alone and have accepted my decisions and Joe's as well,

he now makes up his own mind. Recently Joe's class was selected by a London hospital as a trial group to see how many children of that age suffer from allergies. The whole class had some kind of allergy except Joe who has none at all. His friends actually said "there must be something wrong with you as we all have allergies and you don't!"

BIBLIOGRAPHY

1   Ethel Douglas Hume, *Pasteur Exposed – Germs Genes Vaccines,* Bodyreal

2   *Immunisation Against Infectious Disease,* HMSO, London 1992

3   J. H. Playfair, *Immunology at a Glance,* Blackwell Scientific Publications

4   Peter Wingate, *The Penguin Medical Encyclopedia,* Penguin

5   Peter Parish, *Medical Treatments – The Benefits and Risks,* Penguin

6   R. E. Dudgeon, *The Lesser Writings of Samuel Hahnemann,* B. Jain Publishers (Put.) Ltd

7   G Macpherson (Ed.), *Black's Medical Dictionary, 37th Edition,* A & C Black

8   Jennifer Meek, *Immune Power,* Optima

9   R. J. Harrison, *Textbook of Medicine,* Unibooks

10   Sir MacFarlane Burnett & David O White, *National History of Infectious Diseases,* Cambridge University Press

11   Harris L Coulter & Barbara Loe Fisher, *A Shot in the Dark,* Avery Publishing Group

12   Julius P Kreier & Richard J Mortensen, *Infection, Resistance & Immunity,* Harper & Row

13   1994 Red Book, *Report of the Committee on Infectious Diseases,* American Academy of Pediatrics

14   Jamie Murphy, *What Every Parent Should Know about Childhood Immunization,* Earth Healing Products

15   Wynn McTaggart, *The Vaccination Bible, What Doctors Don't Tell You*

16   Viera Scheibner, PhD, *Vaccination – A Medical Assault on the Immune System,* Self Published (available through The Informed Parent).

17.   Dr Jean Elminper, *Discovering Real Medicine,* Element Books.

ORGANISATIONS THAT CAN BE CONTACTED FOR SUPPORT AND FURTHER INFORMATION:

THE INFORMED PARENT:
Magda Taylor, P.O. Box 870, Harrow, Middx, HA3 7UW,
Tel: 020 861 1022.
The Informed Parent provides information, leaflets and a newsletter.

JABS:
Jackie Fletcher,
1 Gawsworth Road, Golbourne, Warrington, Cheshire, WA3 3RF,
Tel: 01942 713565 Fax: 01942 201323.
JABS puts out a quarterly newsletter with information on vaccinations and side effects.

VACCINE VICTIM SUPPORT:
Oliver Price, 27 Malcom Grove, Rednall, Birmingham, B45 9BS,
Tel: 0121-243 7759.
Provides help, information and support to parents of vaccination damaged children trying to claim compensation.

VACCINATION AWARENESS U.K.
178 Mansfield Road, Nottingham, NG1 3HW,
Tel: 0115 950 3858.
This is a charity again providing information on vaccination damage but also is very involved in looking at similar problems for animals.

HEALTH ACTION NETWORK:
John Andrews, P.O. Box 43, Hull, HU1 1AA,
Tel: 01482-562079
Provides information on vaccinations for children and animals and will post information packs on request.

INDEX

Bronchitis – 28, 54

Broncho-pneumonia – 29, 40, 44, 63

Caesarean – 52

Calcium Carbonate – 64

Calcium Phosphate – 13

Calcium Sulphate – 51

Canada – 7

Cancer – 24, 35, 54

Candida – 4, 16

Catarrh – 8, 9, 28, 30, 37, 43, 51, 52

Chicken Pox – 7, 29, 37, 49

Chinchona Bark – 2

Chronic Enterocolitis – 21

Clostridium Tetani – 45

Colcus Cacti – 43

Conjunctivitis – 28, 30, 31, 43

Constitutional – 10, 12, 37, 49, 50, 51, 64

Consumption – 61

Convulsions – 28, 44, 46, 55, 59

Cortisone – 13, 36, 51

Cri Encephalique – 44

Crohn's Disease – 21, 26, 33

Croup – 28, 49, 50

Cyanosis – 40

Cytotoxic T-cells – 21

Diabetes – 19, 31, 54

Diarrhoea – 11, 34, 36, 37, 65

Dilution – 2

Diphtheria – 25, 40, 41, 49,55

DPT – 6, 7, 12, 13, 33, 37, 46, 48, 49, 50, 51, 52, 55, 58, 64

Drug layer – 12, 13

Ear infections – 3, 6, 8, 9, 28, 34, 36, 37, 49, 63, 65

Eardrum – 9, 36

Eczema – 12, 35, 36, 48, 49, 50, 51, 64, 65

Empyema – 29

Encephalitis – 29

Encephalomyelitis – 16, 31, 32

Enteritis – 33, 52

Erythema Nodosum – 62

Erythrocytes – 19

Euphrasia – 30

Eustachian tubes – 8, 9

Exanthematous – 28

Ferrum Phosphoricum – 33

If you would like to order extra copies of "An Educated Decision" please fill in the form below:

Name: _____

Address:_____

_____

Town: _____

County: _____ Post Code: _____

Price £9.99 per copy plus £1.00 p&p

Please make cheques out to C.J. Head and post your order to:

Christina J. Head MCH RsHom ng Company
The Lavender Hill Publishing Co.
PO Box 141
Reigate
Surrey RH2 9YT
Tel. 01737 762497

For all enquiries including trade orders please ring: 0207 978 4519 or 01737 216428 or email: chead@lavenderpublishing.fsnet.co.uk or visit our web site www.aneducateddecision.com